"As a young mother, many of us face the hard choice of whether to work or not. Most of us want to stay home with our children when they are little. Let's face it they need us and no one can replace a mother. If you have to work, working from home is a much better option. Randi Millward's book *100 Income Streams for Full-time Moms* is a great resource for finding work at home.

- Margie Robertson-Toone
author of **Mama's Country Cooking**

"You have got to be one of the most inspirational women I know. Your insight in to these money saving/earning ventures astounds me! This book, I'm sure will be a wonderful asset to anyone's library! I've stayed home with my kids now for over 15 years. I've authored a newsletter for stay-at-home-moms, home based data entry, tutoring, babysitting, sewing/knitting/crocheting/painting things for sale as well as a road side vegetable stand. With all of these ventures there have been some successes, some failures, but mostly a sense of well being knowing that not only am I contributing to my husband's income, but all the cost of my materials are tax deductible. I would highly recommend your book to anyone who is looking for some ideas on how to make some extra money so they can stay home with their children."

- Regina Graham
Regina's Aprons N Things

Disclaimer: This book is designed to provide ideas and information about possible income streams. Every effort has been made to make it as complete and accurate as possible, but no warranty or fitness is implied or included.

This book and its contents are not legal advice. If you desire legal counsel, consult a lawyer.

No profit is guaranteed from using any of the information herein.

It is the sole responsibility of the reader to research all applicable federal, state, and local laws, rules, and regulations regarding the income streams and any aspects of the income streams mentioned in this book. It is the sole responsibility of the reader to render any and all applicable taxes according to government standards.

The author and publisher are not liable for any loss or damages sustained by, or resulting from, any information contained in this book.

ISBN 10: 0-9827334-1-0
ISBN 13: 978-0-9827334-1-7

All content of this book is copyright 2010 by Expressions of Perceptions ™ and Randi Lynn Millward.

All rights reserved. No part of this book may be copied, transmitted, sold, translated, photocopied, or otherwise reproduced by any means without written permission from the author and/or publisher.

Cover photo is property of Expressions of Perceptions ™ and Randi Lynn Millward and may not be copied, transmitted, sold, translated, photocopied, or otherwise reproduced by any means without written permission from the author and/or publisher.

100 Income Streams for Full-time Moms: Because Your *Children* are Your Full-time Job

By Randi Lynn Millward

Thanks & Dedication

First and foremost, to God who has given me talents and abilities, whether or not I fully develop them, and Jesus Christ, my Lord and Savior.

To my incredibly supportive husband, Travis, without whom I wouldn't have my wonderful children who provide me with so much inspiration.

To my amazing children, Aurora, Mercy, and Linkin, who provide me with more ideas and inspiration than I could ever possibly use and who never fail to bring a smile to my face. I love you more than words can say.

To my mother, Cindy, who is never anything less than my biggest fan.

To all full-time moms, families, and children who may benefit from this book in some way. May God abundantly bless your faith, family, and finances.

Advance Praise for:
100 Income Streams for Full-time Moms:
Because Your *Children* are Your Full-time Job

"What a great resource for moms who are just starting out on their work-at-home journey. Randi has packed this book full of ideas and step-by-step instructions to help readers launch at-home careers. Randi has not only done a great job putting this resource together, she's also the perfect example that her book does work as she used these same techniques in building her own business."

- Jill Hart
Christian Work at Home Moms®
co-author of **So You Want to Be a Work-at-Home Mom**
www.CWAHM.com

"Randi has created an excellent source for ideas to create your own business. With a little ingenuity and research you will be on your way to creating income in practically no time. Her estimates on time required, potential income, what to do with the children, and additional resources for research will help you choose an appropriate business that will bring you income while still meeting your family obligations. It's a win win proposition.

For over 20 years I have been self employed using many of the ideas that Randi has suggested. My businesses have grown and morphed to give me the flexibility to take care of my family and home. As my children's needs changed, I changed my business to accommodate their needs. When my children grew and left home my business became a successful full time venture. I STILL have the flexibility and income to visit the grandchildren or to help my aging parents. Being my own boss has really worked for me. You can make it work for you thanks to Randi's book to get you started."

- Catherine Machnics
Catherine Machnics Fine Interior Painting
http://cathypaints.spaces.live.com

"What a wonderful book! In this economy, many have already reduced their expenses to a bare minimum. The only way then to meet these necessary expenses is to increase income. Randi has given 100 common sense, practical ideas that work. Anyone seeking additional income can find one or two good ideas and begin to implement them right away, knowing time-wise, expense-wise, and income-wise what to reasonably expect.

This is a **MUST-READ** for any person (man or woman) at any stage of life (no children, young children, or grown children) who seeks to increase their income for whatever reason.

I will be recommending this book to everyone who attends one of my debt-elimination workshops."

- Bob Marette
author of *From A Millstone To A Milestone*
How to Get Out of Debt in 5 – 7 Years, Including Mortgage
and
SCRIPTURAL CALENDAR: A Daily Guide To Help
You Hide God's Word In Your Heart
www.FinancialHealthFair.org

"I am impressed with Randi's ability to "think outside the box." So many mothers want to stay at home and still provide an income, yet feel their options are limited to what everyone else is already doing. Many times those options are unfeasible for a full-time mom. Randi not only provides some very uncommon income streams in her book, she gives you tools to brainstorm ideas that are unique to YOU!"

- Angie Nelson
The Work at Home Wife
ASN Virtual Services
www.theworkathomewife.com

Table of Contents

Introduction 11

The Income Streams..17
1. Accounting..19
2. Affiliate Link Advertising...21
3. Animal Breeding...23
4. Authoring Books...27
5. Baby Proofing...31
6. Babysitting..35
7. Bartender for Hire...37
8. Billboard Rental..39
9. Birth Doula...43
10. Bookkeeping...47
11. Catering..49
12. Children's Entertainer..53
13. Clicking at Paid to Click Websites......................................55
14. Computer Maintenance and Repair.....................................57
15. Conflict Coaching..59
16. Consulting..63
17. Custom Cake Baking and Decorating.................................65
18. Data Entry..69
19. Dating Coaching..71
20. Daycare Provider...75
21. Delivery Driver..77
22. Direct Sales..79
23. Dog Obedience Training...83
24. Dog Walking..85
25. Editing..87
26. Fact Checking..89
27. Fitness Instruction..91
28. Flipping Houses...93
29. Florist...97
30. Flyer Distribution Services..99
31. Food Critic...103

32. Forex Trading..105
33. Freelance Copywriting..109
34. Freelance Writing for Periodicals....................................113
35. Gardening and Farming..117
36. Get Paid to Drive Advertising..121
37. Gift Basket Business..123
38. Gift Wrapping..127
39. Health & Wellness Coaching...131
40. Home Staging..135
41. Housekeeping..137
42. Housesitting..141
43. Human Intelligence Tasks...145
44. Illustrating..147
45. Interior Decorating..149
46. Interpreting...153
47. Inventing..157
48. Land Surveying..159
49. Laundromat Owner..161
50. Laundry Services..165
51. Life Coaching...169
52. Locksmithing..173
53. Massage Therapy..177
54. Mobile Search Guide..181
55. Motivational Speaking..183
56. Movie Reviewing..187
57. Multi-level Marketing...189
58. Music Lessons..191
59. Mystery Shopping..193
60. Notary Services..197
61. Note Brokering...201
62. Online Auctions and Fixed-price Listings....................205
63. Online Customer Service Representative....................209
64. Online Paid Surveys...211
65. Operating a Paid to Click Website...............................213
66. Packing..215
67. Paid Membership Websites...219
68. Painting...221
69. Party Planning...223
70. Personal Chef..227

71. Personal Scrapbooking..229
72. Personal Shopping..233
73. Pet Sitting...235
74. Photography...237
75. Placemat Advertising...239
76. Postpartum Doula...243
77. Potty Training...245
78. Private Investigating..249
79. Private Security Guard...251
80. Real Estate Agent...253
81. Real Estate Appraisals..255
82. Rental Properties..257
83. Restaurant Dessert Baking...261
84. Resume Writing..265
85. Reupholstery...269
86. Sewing..271
87. Snow Removal..273
88. Stand-up Comedy...275
89. Tanning Salon...277
90. The Stock Market..279
91. Translating..281
92. Travel Agent...283
93. Tutoring..287
94. Vehicle Detailing..289
95. Videography...291
96. Virtual Assistant...293
97. Website Content Writing..295
98. Website Creation & Maintenance...............................297
99. Wedding Planning..301
100. Wild Game Processing...305

Conclusion..309

Personal Income Stream Assessment......................311

Sample Personal Income Stream Assessment.........313

About The Author...317

Introduction

I am a full-time mom. I'm very blessed to be able to stay at home to raise my children. We aren't rich. We weren't given any trust funds. My husband has a good job, though it's not a job that's going to make him rich. It's a job that doesn't require a college degree. It doesn't provide a 6-figure income or performance bonuses, but we make it work for us – a family of five.

So many times, other mothers have told me that they wish they could afford to stay at home with their children like I do. When they said that, I always thought *you can if you want to. Just handle your finances better. Cut some expenses. Live without some luxuries.* In reality though, sometimes no matter how hard you try, you just can't save enough money by cutting expenses to be able to live on one income. There are necessary expenses that you can cut back on.

There are also expenses that you shouldn't cut back on. You shouldn't sacrifice nutrition in your children's diets for the sake of saving money, you shouldn't sacrifice medical checkups to save the cost of co-pays, and you can't make your children just wear last season's fashions if they've clearly grown two sizes since then.

So in instances where saving isn't the answer, what is? Earning. Earning is the answer. But earning doesn't have to be a full-time-away-from-home type of job. You may not even need a full-time income to be able to afford to stay home. Perhaps you only need to earn a hundred dollars per month to make staying home feasible, maybe you need a few hundred, or maybe you do need a full-time income.

Perhaps you're already a stay-at-home mom, but you want to earn an income, too. You might be struggling financially, or you might just want a little extra spending money or money for a family vacation.

No matter what your situation, if saving isn't providing you with the amount of money that you want or need, maybe it's time you tried earning. I know, I know, you don't want to leave your children. The good news is that you don't have to.

You can be a full-time mom and earn an income, too. You can work as little or as much as you'd like. You can work inside your home or outside of your home. You can be your own boss. You can have a flexible schedule. You can earn an income from something you enjoy. All of that is possible.

In this book, you'll find 100 possible income streams that I've chosen to write about specifically for full-time moms. You could choose one that is listed, or you could create your own. You could turn virtually any hobby, niche, or expertise into a stream of income. With a hundred possible income streams listed, if you can't find at least one that's right for you, you should at least be able to use the information as a guide to help you think of one that is.

About the Income Streams

The income streams listed are not get-rich-quick schemes. They're businesses that could earn you a modest to full-time income, depending on the amount of effort you put into them.

Not all of the businesses will work in every area of the country. Be sure to factor in your location when determining the income stream that would be best for you.

Different income streams may work better for mothers of children of certain ages. Some may work better for mothers of teenagers, some for mothers of toddlers, some for mothers of school age children, and some for mothers of children of any age.

For each income stream listed, I've provided a brief overview that explains what it is and suggestions for what you could do with your children while you work. When possible and/or applicable, I've also listed an estimate of the amount of time you'll spend working, an estimate of income, an estimate of any possible initial investment that may be needed, ideas for how to advertise, and additional information and/or resources that may be helpful for that particular income stream.

As stated above, the explanations of the income streams are brief. They are just examples. With writing about a hundred of them, there wasn't enough room to go into great detail about each one. If the income stream appeals to you, you may need to research it further, but you'd be doing that anyway if you chose it as your new source of income.

The suggestions for what to do with your children when you work are also just examples and suggestions. Every child and family has different needs. You'll decide what to do with your children based on what you feel is right for them and for your family.

The estimated time you'll spend working is just an estimate and an example. It won't be the same for everyone. It's just a ballpark figure. There are too many factors to tell you exactly how much time you'll spend working. Even two people doing the exact same work may work at different speeds, thus making their work hours different.

The estimate of income is also just an estimate and example. Again, it's just a ballpark figure that will be different for everyone. Prices for nearly everything vary from state to state, city to city, and business to business. A huge factor in projecting your income is your location.

The estimated investment needed may or may not include actual monetary amounts. Since prices for products and services vary by location, it may just list supplies or other materials. The cost of advertising isn't listed in the section on the initial investment needed. Methods and prices of advertising vary by location. You can choose whatever venue of advertising you would like to use and can afford, if advertising is even necessary.

The section of additional information for each income stream may include websites, books, or just an extra tip or two. I do not endorse any resource listed. They are listed as possible sources for more information about the income streams. I can't guarantee their accuracy. There are numerous more resources available besides the ones I listed. Feel free to find your own.

I've conducted the research and put forth the effort to introduce these income streams to you. You'll do the research and put forth the effort to make them your own.

Regulations

Different income streams may have different laws, rules, regulations, and requirements. Because those regulations can vary by location, you'll need to check with the proper government authority where you live to find out about any necessary training, licensing, permits, certifications, insurance, or other requirements for your chosen income stream. You'll want to be in full compliance with all local, state, and national laws that pertain to your business.

If necessary, you could consult with a small business attorney.

Additional Tips

Networking

Once you've gotten started with your new income stream, you could begin networking to find more contacts and possibly generate more clients or customers. Whether you're looking for customers, clients, support, encouragement, advice, or resources, networking could be helpful to you. You could join your local Chamber of Commerce. You could network online. You could even befriend other entrepreneurs in your area. All of those methods could be helpful to keep your business going.

Priorities

I believe the key to any successful business is having your priorities straight. The method I recommend, and the only one I can rely on, is to put God first, family second, and your business after those two. This probably doesn't sound like a traditional business book with me telling you that your source of income should take a backseat to other things, but that is the order in which I believe priorities should be. I am a firm believer in Proverbs 16:3.

I also believe in the Biblical principle of giving and it been given unto you even more than you gave. I believe in tithing. If it's difficult to think of giving ten percent of your income away, you could think of it as keeping ninety percent for yourself.

If you're a full-time mom, your family is probably already a priority over your income. Don't forget to keep it that way even if you start to get busy. Remind yourself why you chose your job. If you find yourself getting so busy that you're neglecting your family, take a break, work fewer hours, or hire some help. Your children are only young once, so cherish their youth. Remember, you were probably a wife, a mother, a sister, a daughter, an aunt, a niece, a granddaughter, and an in-law before you were the businesswoman that you became after starting your newly-found income stream.

Don't forget to nurture those relationships. After all, money doesn't seem as important when you don't have anyone to share it with, spend it on, or talk to about it.

Happy customers or clients should be a priority, too. After all, your business depends on them. Great customer service is one of the main reasons for return business, and happy customers or clients may even recommend your business to others.

Keeping Records

Make sure to keep a record of all of your business transactions. You'll need them for tax purposes. Record your income and expenses. Some donations or contributions may be tax-deductible.

Earning More

If your chosen income stream won't earn you the income you desire, you could add more income streams until you reach your goal. You don't have to settle on just one. As long as you can juggle multiple businesses, along with the rest of your life, there's no reason why you'd have to limit yourself to just one. If you wanted, and were able, you could be a full-time mom and a part-time SEO consultant who rents billboard space, sells cosmetics, and earns royalties on the sales of a book written a couple years ago.

You could just think of it as diversification. Some people diversify their investments to minimize potential losses. You make an investment of time, energy, and possibly money in your businesses, so your businesses are your investments. You could think of having multiple businesses as diversifying your investments, not to minimize losses, but to maximize gains.

Your other option would be to expand your business and hire help. Although paying for help would be another expense, the added income from expanding your business should still allow you to increase your profits without encroaching on your family time.

The Income Streams

Accounting

What You'll Do:
As an accountant, you'll be responsible for the financial records of the clients for which you are working. You'll create the income statements and balance sheets for businesses. You could be in charge of a company's payroll. You may prepare tax returns, conduct audits, or perform other financial duties.

Although accounting is similar to bookkeeping, you need formal training to be an accountant.

What to do with Your Children:
You could work from home when you have free time from which you won't be distracted. You could work while your children are napping, in bed at night, at school, at sports practice, or at a playdate. If you'll be needing a large amount of time to work while your children are home, you could have your husband care for them, or you could hire a babysitter to supervise them while you work.

Estimated Time Required:
The time required will depend on how many clients you have and what their financial needs may be. Without knowing those factors, there is no reliable estimate for the time required. It could be full-time, but if you accept and decline clients based on the amount of time you have available to work, you could work as many or as few hours as you'd like.

Estimated Income:
Around the time of this writing, I believe the pay rate was in the ballpark of $27 per hour. Pay rates vary in different parts of the country and are generally dependent on the various duties you perform. If you worked 6 hours per day, 3 days per week, at a rate of $25 per hour, you'd earn $1800 per month. That's just an example though. Your income will depend on your pay rate and the number of hours you work.

Estimated Investment Needed:
You will need formal training for this business. The cost for that will vary depending on where and how you receive your training. You may earn one or multiple certifications. The requirements for receiving a license vary by state. At the time of this writing though, the Uniform Certified Public Accountant examination is required by all states.

Advertising:
You could put an ad in the telephone book and newspaper. You could hand out business cards to everyone you run into. After all, everyone has to file their taxes. You could also leave business cards at banks, investment firms, and other financial institutions.

Additional Information and Resources:
Check the requirements in your state for becoming an accountant.
Some websites that you may find helpful are listed below.
- www.en.wikipedia.org/wiki/Accountant
- www.workathomenoscams.com/work-from-home-companies
- www.pennfostercollege.edu/accounting
- www.wisegeek.com/what-is-an-accountant.htm
- www.aicpa.org

Affiliate Link Advertising

What You'll Do:
　　With affiliate link advertising, you'll simply place links to other websites on your website. If someone clicks on the link and makes a purchase on that site, you'll earn a percentage of the sale price.
　　There is a multitude of companies that offer affiliate link commissions, from dating sites to mass market retailers. You could place as many links on your site as you want and receive commissions from all of them.
　　You will need to have a website on which to put the links though. It could be any type of site. It could be your personal blog, a direct sales site, or virtually any other site. The companies whose links you'll be posting on your website will supply you with banners, buttons, or some other form of link for you to place on your site so that they can track the sales your website is generating them. Your commissions will usually be paid on a monthly basis.

What to do with Your Children:
　　Once you have the links on your website, you won't need to alter your routine at all. They'll just be on your website for anyone who visits your website to click on. Your time with your children probably won't be affected at all.

Estimated Time Required:
　　After the links are on your website, you probably won't need to spend any time at all on this income stream, other than occasionally clicking on the links yourself to make sure they're still in working order.

Estimated Income:
　　Your income will depend on the number of visitors to your site that click on the affiliate links and make purchases on them. It will also depend on the purchase prices of the items sold and the

percentage of the sales prices that you'll be earning. There is no reliable estimate of income for this income stream without knowing those factors.

Estimated Investment Needed:
    If you don't already have a website, you'll need to buy or build one. You could pay a professional, or you could use a free website builder to build your own site. You could pay to advertise your site online if you wanted to, but you could register it with search engines for free.
    Your commissions depend on you bringing visitors to your website though, so you may or may not want to pay to bring traffic to your site.

Advertising:
    You probably won't advertise for this anymore than you already advertise your website.
    To get the affiliate links, you won't advertise. You'll just go to the websites that you want to promote, look for their affiliate link, and apply to be an affiliate marketer with them. Once they check out your site, they'll let you know whether or not you're accepted to be an affiliate marketer for their business.

Additional Information and Resources:
    Although I don't endorse any sites listed, the following websites may be helpful for you for this income stream.
- www.freeservers.com
- www.webs.com
- www.affiliatetips.com
- www.chemistry.com/glp/affiliate/1000
- www.affiliates.walmart.com/aff_home.jsp
- www.affiliate-program.amazon.com
- www.drugstore.com/templates/stackdept/default.asp?catid=14230

Animal Breeding

What You'll Do:

As a professional animal breeder, you'll care for animals' overall well-being while encouraging them to reproduce. First, you must decide what animal you would like to breed. You could breed dogs, cats, cattle, pigs, chickens, mice, or most any other animal.

To make the most profit, I recommend breeding purebred animals since they sell for more than mixed-breed animals. Your initial investment to purchase a male and a female purebred will be higher than if you were to buy mixed-breeds, but since you'll be able to sell them for a higher price, it should be worth your investment.

You could breed dogs for trainers to enter in pet shows. You could breed mice for pet stores to sell as snake food. You could breed cattle for farmers. You could also breed purebred or mixed-breed cats and dogs for pet stores to sell or to sell yourself just as family pets.

Of course your responsibilities will depend on what kind of animals you choose to breed, but in general, you'll need to feed and water them, arrange veterinary care, and make sure they have a clean, safe environment.

To sell the animals, you could sell them from your home, or you could contact pet stores to see if they'd be interested in selling the animals at their stores.

What to do with Your Children:

Your children may really enjoy you having this kind of job. They could help with feeding and brushing, but they may be opposed to shoveling manure or emptying litter boxes.

As long as you feel as though your children would be safe around the animals, you won't need to arrange for childcare. If you don't want your children around the animals, if it's even possible to keep them away, perhaps your spouse could care for your children while you tend to the animals.

Estimated Time Required:
The time you spend working will depend on the kind of animals you choose to breed. How often will they need fed and watered? How often will they need to be groomed and bathed? Will you have to drive them to the vet, or will the vet be coming to you? Will they need to be walked?

Without knowing the number and species of animals you'll be breeding, there's probably no reliable way to estimate the time you'll need to devote to this business.

Estimated Income:
Your income will depend on the number animals you breed, the species, the amount of offspring they produce, the sale price of each animal, and the cost of their care. There isn't even an estimated range of income for you without knowing those factors.

Estimated Investment Needed:
Of course you'll need to invest in a male and a female of the species you choose to breed. The cost of that will depend on the species of animal you've chosen.

You may or may not need a breeding license. The cost for licenses may vary by state.

You'll need to purchase food for the animals, possibly water bowls or troughs, and shelter for the animals if you don't already have it. You'll also be responsible for the costs of any and all medical care for the animals.

Advertising:
You could place an ad in the newspaper when the baby animals are old enough to leave their mother. You could call pet stores to offer them the option to purchase the animals. You could hang flyers at veterinarians' offices, toy stores, feed stores, or businesses that may have customers that would be interested in the animals you're breeding.

Additional Information and Resources:
Don't forget to check into license requirements and laws in your state regarding animal breeding and sales.

A few websites that may be helpful for you for your animal breeding business are listed below.
- http://www.jobmonkey.com/animaljobs/animal-breeders.html
- http://www.payscale.com/research/US/Job=Animal_Breeder/Salary
- http://www.careerplanner.com/Job-Descriptions/Animal-Breeders.cfm

Authoring Books

What You'll Do:
    As a book author, you'll write fiction or nonfiction books of any genre. You could write romance novels, children's books, how-to books, reference books, mysteries, or any other type of book that you'd like. You could write about anything that you're interested in or knowledgeable about.
    You could submit your book to traditional publishers, self-publish, or pay a vanity publisher to publish your book. After your book is in print, you could earn royalties on it for years to come. Unless your book is a best-seller though, you probably won't earn enough royalties to live off of from just one book, but you could always write more until you're happy with your royalty income.

What to do with Your Children:
    You could work from home anytime you have free time. You could work while your children are napping, in bed at night, at school, at sports practice, at a playdate, or even watching television or playing a game. If you're writing children's books, you could sit at the table with your children and get their input while you work.

Estimated Time Required:
    The time required will depend on the types of books you're writing. Books that require you to perform research will require more time than books that don't. Children's books may require less time than novels. There's no real estimate for the time required, but unless you're working with a publisher that has given you a strict deadline, you can spend as much or as little time working as you'd like.

Estimated Income:
    Your income will depend on the method of publication you use, the sale price of your book, the number of books that you sell, and the percentage of royalties that you earn per sale. There is no

reliable estimate of income for this income stream without knowing those factors.

Estimated Investment Needed:

There's probably no mandatory investment for this business. You should have a computer on which to type your manuscript, but most people already have that. If you're hiring an illustrator, you'll be responsible for the costs of that. If you're self-publishing or paying a vanity publisher to publish your book, you'll be responsible for that cost, too.

Traditional publishers don't charge you to publish your book. Self-publishing could probably cost you anywhere from a couple hundred dollars and up, depending on the publisher and the genre of your book. Vanity publishers usually charge many thousands of dollars.

Advertising:

You won't advertise that you're writing books. If you're not self-publishing, you'll send query letters and/or your manuscript to publishers to see if they'd be interested in publishing your book.

Once your book is in print, traditional publishers will probably advertise for you. If you're self-publishing or using a vanity publisher, you may be responsible for your own advertising. Either way, your book will most likely be listed for sale at various online retailers, such as Amazon.com.

Book signings are a great method of advertising. I also recommend sending review copies to various periodicals that may print a review of your book. Creating a website and registering it with online search engines could be helpful, too. You could also rent a booth at book shows, hand out business cards, and tell your friends and family members to spread the word.

Additional Information and Resources:

Some resources that you may find helpful are listed below.
- www.CreateSpace.com
- www.LightningSource.com
- www.fabjob.com/ChildAuthor.asp
- www.ehow.com/how_2057347_become-published-author.html

- How I Write: Secrets of a Bestselling Author by Janet Evanovich and Ina Yalof
- Your First Novel: An Author Agent Team Share the Keys to Achieving Your Dream by Ann Rittenberg and Laura Whitcomb
- Yes! You Can Learn How to Write Children's Books, Get Them Published, and Build a Successful Writing Career by Nancy I. Sanders
- Writing with Pictures: How to Write and Illustrate Children's Books by Uri Shulevitz
- The Magic of Writing: How to Write and Publish the Book that is Inside You by Linda Falkner
- 2010 Writer's Market Deluxe by Robert Lee Brewer
- 2010 Novel & Short Story Writer's Market by Alice Pope
- Christian Writers' Market Guide 2010 by Sally E. Stuart

Babyproofing

What You'll Do:
As a professional babyproofer, you'll be responsible for making the baby's environment safe. You'll meet with the parents at their home and take a tour of the residence to identify potential hazards. They can point out to you any area in their house where they have safety concerns. You'll point out potentially dangerous areas to them. Take a notebook and pen with you to note all of the areas that need babyproofed.

If you've babyproofed your own home, you should have an idea of what needs babyproofed. Looking at baby safety products in catalogs will also offer ideas, perhaps even new ones that weren't thought of when you babyproofed your own home.

You can put together a portfolio of babyproofing supplies with the amount you'll charge for them. Of course you'll put a slight markup on the products. After the parents decide what all they'd like, after you guide them through their decisions if necessary, you'll order all of the supplies they desire. You'll probably require a deposit at this point. Once you receive the supplies, you'll return to the residence and install the items that need to be installed.

You'll probably install cabinet door locks, appliance locks, and safety gates. You may install toilet lid locks and corner cushions. Some safety items, such as bath seats, won't need installation. You'll just deliver them, and the parents will use them as necessary.

After you're done, you'll collect the balance of the amount due. You could ask for a letter of recommendation to keep in your portfolio to show potential clients.

Make sure you're very thorough with this job. You may want to have your clients sign a waiver releasing you from liability if they decline an item you suggest and it results in their child being injured. The waiver should also state that your services improve the safety of the environment but do not guarantee that their children will never get hurt. You may want to consult an attorney for legal advice regarding the waiver and any potential liability you may have.

What to do with Your Children:
Your children should not come with you when you go to your clients' homes. If you can focus, it shouldn't hurt for you to place the orders for the baby safety items online while your children are at home though.

You could have your spouse or a babysitter care for your children while you meet with clients, evaluate their safety needs, and install the safety items. If your children are older, you could work while they are in school, at a playdate, or at sports practice.

Estimated Time Required:
The time required would depend on the size of the residence and the number of potential hazards. Meeting with clients, evaluating their homes, and helping them decide on the items to order could take around 2 to 4 hours, depending on how decisive the parents are. Installing the items could take anywhere from a day to a few days, depending on the size of the residence. There is no ballpark answer for the time required for this income stream without knowing those factors. Just estimate it by the amount of time it took to babyproof your own home.

Estimated Income:
Your income will depend on the number of clients you have and the amount of time it takes to babyproof their home.

If you charged $50 for the initial home safety evaluation, $25 per hour to install the safety items, and averaged $50 per order in markups for the safety items, a job that took you 8 hours to install all the safety products would earn you $300.

Of course the amount you charge will depend on the going rate in your area, but you could probably make a decent income from this no matter where you live.

Estimated Investment Needed:
I recommend that you pay to meet with a lawyer for advice on your liability and to have him draw up a waiver. Other than that, you would probably spend less than $10 to make your portfolio of

products offered. You'll need money, or at least a credit card, to pay for the safety products ordered unless you charge your clients for them up front. I would recommend charging for them up front, but if you don't charge the entire price, you should at least have them make a small deposit. You'll also need any tools that may be necessary for installing the baby safety items.

Advertising:
Word of mouth would be great advertising for this business. Once you've got one happy client, you can be sure she'll tell other parents about your services.

To get started, you could leave business cards and hang flyers at day care centers, pediatricians' offices, family restaurants, toy stores, and grocery stores. You could also advertise in the newspaper and place an ad in the telephone book.

Additional Information and Resources:
Some websites that you may find helpful for ordering baby safety products are listed below.
- www.OneStepAhead.com
- www.BabyMallOnline.com
- www.BabySafetyStore.com
- www.BabySafetySite.com

You may also be able to register your services online at the following website.
- www.BabyproofingDirectory.com

Babysitting

What You'll Do:
    As a babysitter, you'll be responsible for caring for other people's children, most likely in your home. You'll supervise them to make sure they don't get hurt. You may have to feed them, change their diapers, and put them down for naps. You'll also have to clean up after them.
    Babysitting probably won't be a regularly scheduled event. Most people use babysitters on special occasions and as childcare providers that can be called upon at the last minute or on a whim. For regular childcare, most working parents leave their children at daycare, though some hire a nanny or leave their children with a relative.
    Babysitting is sporadic, but if you're comfortable with flexible hours and flexible pay, you may want to consider it.

What to do with Your Children:
    Your children can stay at home with you and play with the children that you're babysitting. That should keep them all entertained and provide opportunities for your children to socialize with other children.

Estimated Time Required:
    Babysitting is a sporadic income opportunity. Most of the time, you won't have regular hours unless you're hired to babysit during a parent's monthly date night or other regular event. Some months you may work 20 hours, some 40, some none. It all depends on the demand for your service in your area.

Estimated Income:
    Hourly rates vary depending on where you live, the amount of time the children will be at your house, the number of children you'll be babysitting, and the ages of the children.

You would probably earn anywhere from $2 to $12 per hour per child you babysit, depending on the going rate in your area.

Estimated Investment Needed:
There's probably no mandatory investment, but you should obtain clearances, and you should definitely keep your CPR and first aid certifications current. If you don't have your house childproofed, you'll probably want to spend the little bit that it costs to properly childproof.

Advertising:
Just tell your friends and neighbors. Word of mouth is best for babysitting.

Additional Information and Resources:
You may want to consider obtaining clearances and getting references.

Bartender for Hire

What You'll Do:

As a professional bartender for hire, you'll be hired as needed for single events. You'll do things as simple as hand over a bottle of beer to as difficult as mixing specialty drinks. If you have bartending experience, you already have an idea of what it would entail.

If you don't have any bartending experience, you could read a couple books on it, take a bartending class, or even ask a local bar if you could help out one night for free just to get some experience.

Most of the events you'll be hired for will probably be weddings. You'll dress in appropriate attire, show up at the event, stand behind the bar, and give the guests the drinks that they request from the stock of beverages that will be provided for you. If you'll be mixing drinks, you could bring a recipe book with you in case someone requests a drink that you don't know how to make. If you're unsure what to wear, ask beforehand.

You'll also need to know when to stop serving people, and you need to be comfortable telling them that they've had enough and you're cutting them off. Your job will be to provide responsible people with legal beverages, not to encourage intoxication.

You'll be paid by the person who hires you to bartend, and you'll probably also receive tips from the patrons you provide with drinks.

It's safe to assume that you'll work mostly weekend evenings, but you may also work other times, too.

What to do with Your Children:

Your definitely can't bring your children with you for this job, so if your spouse won't be home to watch them, you'll need to have a relative or babysitter care for them. Since you'll be working late at most events, your work nights would be great nights for the children to a have a sleepover at their grandmother's house or with another relative.

Estimated Time Required:
You'll probably be working mostly Friday and Saturday nights. If you work only one 4-hour event every week, that would only be 16 hours per month. That's just an example though. Your hours will vary.

Estimated Income:
Your income will depend on the number of events for which you're hired. Just as an example, if you charge $15 per hour and work two 6-hour shifts per month, you'll earn $180 per month, not including tips. Tips could easily be as much as, or more than, your hourly rate, but they will vary by event.

Estimated Investment Needed:
Although there's probably no mandatory investment needed, it couldn't hurt to buy a book on mixing drinks in case anyone ever requests a drink you don't know how to make. If you don't already own clothing that would be appropriate for the event, you'll need to buy or rent the appropriate attire. To save money on clothing though, you could see if your local Goodwill store or consignment shop has what you need.

Advertising:
Word of mouth would be a good way to get started. I also highly recommend leaving business cards at wedding planners' offices. You could also leave business cards in restaurants, bars, and clubs.
An ad in the telephone book would probably be helpful, too.

Additional Information and Resources:
Numerous books on bartending and mixing drinks can be found online at www.Amazon.com.

Billboard Rental

What You'll Do:

This is an easy way to make some extra money with very minimal effort. All you have to do is build, have your husband build, or hire someone else to build, a plain billboard in a conspicuous location on property that you own. You could use your front yard, your back yard, your side yard, a vacant lot, a grassy area beside a business you own, or even the side of a building.

The more traffic that drives by the billboard location, the more you can charge per month for rent.

Set your desired price per month, and advertise that the billboard is available to rent. Whoever rents the billboard will be responsible for placing their ad on it. They may paint it or affix a ready-made advertisement on it. Get the rental agreement in writing, and collect the rent money every month.

When the customer decides not to renew the rental agreement, just paint over their advertisement, and start advertising the billboard for rent again. You could also state in the rental agreement that the renter is responsible for removing the ad upon termination of the lease.

Depending on the size of the billboard and whether it has one, two, or three sides, you may be able to rent it to multiple customers simultaneously.

Just don't forget to make sure the ads are tasteful and don't promote anything you're opposed to or don't want your children exposed to.

What to do with Your Children:

Your time with your children shouldn't be affected much by this business. You may have to answer a few phone calls and meet with customers to have them sign the rental agreement, but that should be once a month for monthly agreements, and maybe once every six months for longer rentals.

Just return phone calls while your children are napping or playing. You can meet with customers at restaurants or even have them come to your house to sign the agreement. Your children can either be present at home for that, or you could have your husband watch them for an hour or so while you meet your customers at a restaurant.

Estimated Time Required:
Once the billboard is built, you may only need a couple minutes to answer the phone and perhaps an hour to meet a customer to get the rental agreement signed every one to six months. There's hardly any time required for this business.

Estimated Income:
The amount you charge for the monthly rental will depend on the area in which you live, the visibility of the billboard, and the size of the billboard. The more traffic that goes past it, the more you can charge.

You should make a minimum of $100 per month per customer rental. In my area, I believe the going rate is around $300-$400. Check around to see what others in your area are charging. Then, offer a competitive rate.

As a conservative estimate, if you had one billboard with two areas on it available for advertising, if you charged $300 per month per ad, you'd be earning $600 per month. That would be a total of $7,200 per year. That's just an example. Your income will vary.

Estimated Investment Needed:
The initial investment for the cost of lumber, and possibly a carpenter, will vary depending on the size of the billboard. A gallon of paint, paintbrush, and a roller should only cost around $25. You may need to apply for a building permit, too, but the cost of those varies by location.

Advertising:
Once the billboard is built, just paint your phone number on it with an ad stating that the billboard space is currently available for rent. It's sure to catch the eye of those who drive past it.

Additional Information and Resources:
Don't forget to check your local governing authority for laws, rules, and regulations, and for possible building permits you may need.

Birth Doula

What You'll Do:

As a birth doula, your job will be to assist women in the time leading up to childbirth, during labor and delivery, and briefly after the birth. You'll offer emotional, physical, and informational support. You'll meet with each client before the birth to acquaint yourself with her and help her design her birth plan. Once in labor, the woman will call you. You'll be with her throughout the labor and delivery process, most likely in a hospital, offering whatever support and assistance she needs that is in the realm of your capabilities. After the birth, you'll leave when your client wants you to leave. She may ask you to stay for a few more hours, or she may want you to leave right away so she and her husband can bond privately with the new baby. If she needs help nursing, you may stay and offer advice, though most hospitals have a lactation consultant on staff.

You won't be a doctor. You won't delivery the baby. You may explain pain management options and side effects to your client. You may offer comforting words of encouragement to the woman when she's scared or nervous. You may rub her back to help relieve some of the pain of back labor. You may explain what is happening with her body to both her and her husband. You'll be a constant pillar of support, encouragement, and information.

You'll charge a set fee for your services as outlined in the contract that you have your clients sign. You may require them to pay the fee up front or just put down a deposit.

What to do with Your Children:

Your children should definitely not accompany you to work at this job. Since labor is unpredictable, you'll be on-call. You'll need to have reliable childcare plans made in advance. If your husband can't care for the children the entire time you're gone, you'll need to have another relative or a babysitter on-call for when your client goes into labor.

Estimated Time Required:

There is no reliable estimate for this job. Every labor is different. Don't overbook in case you have multiple clients going into labor at the same time. You should probably be on-call for only one client at a time, perhaps for a period of 2 weeks before to one week after her due date.

While at the hospital, you may be there from minutes to hours, or even a full day, depending on how quickly the labor progresses.

On a personal note, my doula was at the hospital with me for about 10 hours for my first birth. My second child was born only 12 minutes after we got to the hospital, and my doula arrived about 3 minutes after that and stayed for about an hour. With my third child, my doula specified only 2 days out of the entire month that she wouldn't be available, and he was born on one of those days. So, as you can see, there is no estimate for the amount of time this job will require of you.

Estimated Income:

Doulas charge hundreds of dollar per client, but they generally only have one client at a time. Check around for rates in your area. You can find information online at DONA.org. Then, offer competitive rates. Just as an example though, if you have 2 clients per month and charge each one $500, you'll earn $1,000 per month, as long as the fee is nonrefundable. If you only require a 50% nonrefundable down payment, you'll only earn half as much if your client doesn't utilize your services after signing the contract.

Estimated Investment Needed:

You may want to check into insurance in case you were to be sued by a client who misunderstood the information you offered or blamed you for an illness or injury.

You should also be certified. The cost of certification may vary.

Advertising:

I recommend placing and ad in your telephone book. You could also leave flyers and business cards at grocery stores, gyms, doctors' offices, spas, hospitals, and birthing centers.

Additional Information and Resources:
For more information, resources, and certification, visit www.DONA.org.

Bookkeeping

What You'll Do:
    As a bookkeeper, you'll be responsible for recording all of the daily financial transactions of the business for which you are keeping records. You'll record all of the day-to-day debits and credits. Bookkeeping is not the same as accounting. Bookkeeping does not technically require an accounting degree. As a bookkeeper, you'll be keeping financial records that an accountant can use to create the income statement and balance sheet.

What to do with Your Children:
    You could work from home when you have free time from which you won't be distracted. You could work while your children are napping, in bed at night, at school, at sports practice, or at a playdate. If you'll be needing a large amount of time to work while your children are home, you could have your husband care for them, or you could hire a babysitter to supervise them while you work.

Estimated Time Required:
    The time required will depend on the number of transactions that are made by the business for which you're keeping books. Companies with more transactions will require more time spent working. Without that information, there is no reliable estimate for the amount of time required, but it probably won't be full-time unless you want it to be. Since you can be a bookkeeper for more than one business, just accept and decline jobs based on the amount of time you have available to work.

Estimated Income:
    Around the time of this writing, I believe the pay rate was in the ballpark of $17 per hour. Pay rates vary in different parts of the country. If you worked 4 hours per day 5 days per week, at a rate of $15 per hour, you'd earn $1200 per month. That's just an example

though. Your income will depend on your pay rate and the number of hours you work.

Estimated Investment Needed:
There's probably no mandatory investment for this business. Experience and a degree in the field of finance would probably be helpful but not an absolute necessity.

Advertising:
You probably won't be advertising much for this job. You could put an ad in the telephone book as an independent bookkeeper. I recommend checking with an employment agency for bookkeeping job listings in your area. You could also search the newspaper employment listings.

Additional Information and Resources:
Some websites that you may find helpful are listed below.
- www.princetonreview.com/Careers.aspx?cid=25
- www.workathomenoscams.com/work-from-home-companies
- www.bookkeeperlist.com
- www.bookkeeperlist.com/salary.shtml
- www.bookkeeperjobs.com
- www.simple.wikipedia.org/wiki/Bookkeeping

Catering

What You'll Do:

As a caterer, you'll be responsible for the preparation of food for the event for which you're providing it. Most of the time, you'll also be responsible for serving the food, too.

In general, you'll be hired to provide food for an event. The person who hires you will decide on the menu, usually with your help and suggestions. You'll then receive a monetary deposit, usually half of the total cost, so that you can buy the groceries needed to prepare the food. You'll cook the food, usually in the kitchen of the location at which you're catering the event. You'll assemble the foods, such as salads, appetizers, buffets, trays of cookies, and crudités. You'll usually be responsible for serving the food, too, which means that you'll probably need to hire servers for the event.

You'll also be responsible for cleaning up afterwards. You'll be expected to leave the kitchen as you found it and to have the dishes washed, dried, and put away.

For small, simple gatherings, you may only be required to make crudités and trays of appetizers and only drop them off for the party without having to stay for the event or participate in the clean-up.

What to do with Your Children:

If your children have reached adolescence, they may make great servers. If not, you'll need to leave them at home with their father, another relative, or a babysitter.

Estimated Time Required:

The amount of time you'd spend catering an event would depend on the variety and complexity of dishes you have to prepare, the number of people you'll be feeding, and how long the event is expected to last. It may take you 4 hours per event, it may take you 8 hours per event. Your hours will vary by event.

Since you'll have the freedom to choose which events to cater and which to pass on to someone else, you'll be able to work only when the event would fit into your schedule. You could cater one event per month or one event per week. You can just work when you're available.

Estimated Income:
Since you'll decide how many events to cater per month, and since the size of the events will vary, your income will vary from month to month.

As a conservative estimate, if you cater one 2-hour event with 20 guests per month, charging $12.50 per person, but only spending $6 on food per person, after paying 2 servers each $7.50 per hour, you'd earn $100 per month.

Another hypothetical estimate would be catering a 3-hour event for 50 people, charging $22 per person but spending $10 on food per person, and hiring 3 servers at a rate of $10 each per hour. Your income from that event would be $510. Do that twice a month, and your monthly income would be $1,020.

The going rate for catering varies. You could earn hundreds or thousands per month depending on where you live and what events you cater.

Estimated Investment Needed:
You may need to purchase kitchen equipment, serving platters, and containers, depending on what you'll have access to in the kitchens in which you'll be working. If you're serving buffet-style, you may need to purchase warmers, but again, that depends on whether or not they'll already be available to you.

You could invest in some disposable pans to make the clean-up quicker, but if there are already enough pans for you to use, this would be optional.

Since you'll receive a down payment, you'll use it to buy the food.

If you hire servers, you'll be responsible for their wages. You can negotiate their pay, but it must be at least minimum wage.

If you hire a babysitter to care for your kids while you're working, you'll deduct the childcare costs from your earnings, too.

Advertising:

You could send brochures and business cards to local clubs and associations. Word of mouth would be great, too.

You may also be able to get a start by catering a church dinner, a high school alumni banquet, or even a Girl Scout banquet.

An ad in the telephone book could be helpful, too.

Additional Information and Resources:

Check with your local government authority to find out the rules and regulations regarding food sales, businesses, and food safety rules and regulations in your area.

Once you've begun catering, don't forget to get letters of recommendation from clients to use as references for future clients.

Children's Entertainer

What You'll Do:
As a children's entertainer, you'll provide entertainment for children, almost always at birthday parties. Sometimes you may work a family reunion or other event, though.
You could do magic tricks as a magician, make balloon animals as a clown, dress up as a child's favorite cartoon character, put on a puppet show as a puppeteer, or do some other activity that may entertain children.
Entertaining probably won't be a regularly scheduled event. People use entertainers on special occasions only, and business would probably usually be best in the summer.
As a children's entertainer, you'll show up at the party, entertain the children, and maybe even get to eat some birthday cake before leaving. It could be a really fun job!

What to do with Your Children:
If your children are invited to the party, you can bring them with you. If not, you'll need to leave them with your spouse, another relative, or a babysitter.

Estimated Time Required:
The parties at which you'll be entertaining will probably only last a few hours, but your entertaining may only last one hour depending on what it is that you'll be doing. You'll mostly work weekends, and may even work more than one party per day, but if you worked 2 parties every other Saturday, that would probably only equal out to 4-8 hours per month.

Estimated Income:
Your rates will depend on the type of entertainment you provide, the going rate in your area, and the amount of time you'll be

working. Check the going rates for clowns, puppeteers, etc. in your area to get an estimate of how much you could earn.

Your rates may vary, but just as an example, if you worked at two parties per month, for one hour each, at a rate of $80 per hour, you'd earn $160 per month.

Estimated Investment Needed:
You should obtain clearances anytime you'll be working with children. You may need to buy or rent a costume. You may need to buy puppets, face paint, balloons, or other supplies. It will depend on your chosen method of entertainment.

Advertising:
Hang flyers and/or leave business cards at daycare centers, toy stores, party supply stores, and grocery store. You could also place an ad in the newspaper and telephone book.

Additional Information and Resources:
You may want to consider obtaining clearances and getting references.

The following resources may provide information that you may find helpful for this business.
- The Birthday Party Business: How to Make a Living As a Children's Entertainer by Bruce Fife
- 101 Hand Puppets: A Beginner's Guide to Puppeteering by Richard Cummings
- Creative Clowning by Bruce Fife, Tony Blanco, Steve Kissell, and Bruce Johnson

Clicking at Paid to Click Websites

What You'll Do:
    At paid to click websites, you'll click on ads and get paid for it. Every time you click, another advertisement will load. You'll continue clicking and viewing advertisements. You'll probably have to view each ad for at least 10 seconds in order to get paid for it, but there should be a timer on the screen to let you know when you can click another ad.
    You'll be paid a set amount per advertisement that you view. You could click at multiple sites. Be careful though. The sites are designed to sell you the products or services being advertised.

What to do with Your Children:
    Since this is an online income stream, you could work from home anytime you have free time. You could work while your children are napping, in bed at night, at school, at sports practice, at a playdate, or even watching television or playing a game.
    You could even click while your children are sitting on your lap watching.

Estimated Time Required:
    The time you spend working will be as little or as much as you'd like. Just click when you want.

Estimated Income:
    Income for this type of income stream varies by site. Check out the payouts on various sites before deciding on a chosen site on which to click.
    You probably won't be able to earn a full-time income by clicking.

Estimated Investment Needed:

You will need a computer and internet access.

Advertising:
You won't advertise. You'll just search online for websites that pay you to click.

Additional Information and Resources:
Some websites that you may find helpful are listed below.
- www.ehow.com/how_4446612_money-paid-click-website.html
- www.paidtoclick.com
- www.getpaidtoclick.top-site-list.com
- www.tempscript.com
- www.bestptc.top-site-list.com

Computer Maintenance and Repair

What You'll Do:
Computer maintenance and repair covers a multitude of tasks. You could clean computers, install wireless network cards, diagnose problems, install printers, repair computers, install DVD burners, download antivirus software, install firewalls, and complete various other tasks. You'll check into any problem that your clients may be having with their computers, or perform any upgrades or updates requested.

You'll most likely charge an hourly rate, with additional charges for any hardware purchases you make for your clients.

What to do with Your Children:
When meeting with clients at their homes, you shouldn't bring your children with you. Go when your children are at school, ask your husband to watch them, drop them off at their grandmother's house, or hire a babysitter.

If you're working on your clients' computers at your house, you'll need to do so when you won't be interrupted, perhaps when your children are at school, taking a nap, or being supervised by your husband or another responsible caregiver.

Estimated Time Required:
The time you spend working will depend on the number of clients you have and the tasks they need you to perform for them.

There is no real estimate for the amount of time you'll spend working. Just accept, postpone, and decline jobs based on the amount of time you want to work.

Estimated Income:
Your income will depend on the demand for your services and the complexity of the tasks you're completing.

Around the time of this writing, you could probably earn around $22 per hour for this job, depending on your experience and your location.

Estimated Investment Needed:
You would need tools, probably mostly screwdrivers, to disassemble and reassemble the computers. You'd probably take a certification course, too. The price for that would vary and could range from hundreds to thousands of dollars, with some schools allowing you to make monthly payments for the price of the course. Check to see if your state requires a certification for this business.

Advertising:
I recommend placing an ad in the telephone book and possibly the newspaper. Hanging flyers in malls and other businesses, putting brochures in brochure racks, and leaving business cards at random locations would get the word out, and so would word of mouth.

Additional Information and Resources:
The following resources may contain information that you may find helpful for this business.
- www.preventiveguru.com
- www.technibble.com/computer-maintenance-technician-salaries-usa-2006
- www.pennfoster.edu/pcrepair/
- www.en.wikipedia.org/wiki/Computer_maintenance
- PC Repair and Maintenance: A Practical Guide by Joel Z. Rosenthal and Kevin Jay Irwin
- A+ Certification PC Maintenance and Repair by Mindworks
- Troubleshooting and Maintaining Your PC All-in-One Desk Reference For Dummies by Dan Gookin

Conflict Coaching

What You'll Do:
    As a conflict coach, your job will be to help your clients improve their conflict management skills. By helping them improve their conflict management abilities, you'll be helping them improve their relationships with others. Though conflicts will still arise in their lives from time to time, with improved skills, your clients may be better able to handle them and attain positive outcomes, compromises, and solutions in those situations. You will probably mostly be helping your clients with marital conflict, but you may also help them with conflicts they have with siblings, parents, bosses, neighbors, coworkers, and other people with whom they have a relationship. It's coaching, not therapy. You'll offer your opinion, words of encouragement, suggestions, or some other type of feedback appropriate for the situation. You will not attempt to diagnose or treat any disorders, but you may suggest counseling if you think it would be beneficial to your clients.
    You'll provide one-on-one sessions with your clients, either over the telephone or in person. You could charge per session or offer a certain number of sessions per week or month and charge a weekly or monthly fee.

What to do with Your Children:
    Since your clients both desire and deserve your undivided attention and discretion, your children should not accompany you to one-on-one sessions. They also should not be heard in the background during telephone sessions. You may need to accommodate various schedules for your clients, but you could try to do most of your coaching while your children are in school, at a playdate, at Sunday school, at sports practice, or napping. You could also have your husband, a babysitter, or another relative supervise your children for you while you work. If your children are adolescents, they should be able to read a book, watch television, or do some other solo activity while you are in another room conducting a telephone session.

Estimated Time Required:

Coaching sessions will probably last 30 minutes, 45 minutes, or one hour, depending on how long you decide to conduct them. You could even offer 10 or 15-minute mini telephone sessions for clients who just have a couple quick questions or need to mildly vent every day or so.

The time you spend coaching will depend on the number of clients you have and the amount of coaching they desire. If you have only 3 clients who each desire two 30-minute sessions per week, that would only be three hours per week.

Decide how much time you want to spend working, and offer sessions of appropriate lengths based on that.

Estimated Income:

You could probably earn around $75-125 per hour, depending on the going rate for coaching in your area. You may even charge as little as $25 per hour to get started. Your income would be difficult to estimate beforehand without knowing the demand for the service. As an extremely conservative example, if you have just 3 clients and charge them each only $120 per month for a weekly 30-minute session, you'll work 6 hours per month and earn a monthly income of $360. That would be $60 per hour. Of course that's just an example though. Your income will vary.

Estimated Investment Needed:

There may be no mandatory investment, but you may want to check into insurance in case you were to be sued by an unhappy client who blames you for an unsuccessful relationship.

You could also invest in conflict coach training. That could probably range from a few hundred dollars to many thousands of dollars. It may or may not be required.

Other than that, you'll need a telephone for phone sessions. If you're conducting face-to-face sessions, you'll probably need an office, or you could meet your clients at a restaurant, park, or some other comfortable location.

Advertising:

I highly recommend placing and ad in your telephone book. Since coaching can be done over the telephone, you could also create a website and register your business on online search engines to reach potential clients hundreds and even thousands of miles away. You could also leave business cards at doctors' offices, flower shops, and even bars.

Additional Information and Resources:

You can find more information at www.stoneandloevy.com.

Consulting

What You'll Do:
 As a consultant, you'll act as an adviser to your clients. You may offer advice, perform hands-on training, or offer your expertise in another manner. The method of advisement you use will depend on the subject on which you're advising.
 To be a consultant, you'll need an area of expertise. There are many different types of consultants. You could be whatever type you are knowledgeable enough to be. You could be a financial consultant, a search engine optimization consultant, an information technology consultant, a training consultant, a marketing consultant, or some other type of consultant. You could help homemakers create a household budget, businesses improve the efficiency of their marketing campaigns, entrepreneurs create a business plan, or managers train their employees. The possibilities are endless, and nearly everyone is a potential client.

What to do with Your Children:
 Since your clients both desire and deserve your undivided attention and discretion, your children should not accompany you when you go to meet your clients. They also should not be heard in the background during telephone conversations. You may need to accommodate various schedules for your clients, but you could try to do most of your consulting while your children are in school or at a playdate. You could also have your husband, a babysitter, or another relative supervise your children for you while you work.

Estimated Time Required:
 The time you'll need to devote to work will depend on the type of consulting you offer and the demand for your services. Without knowing the type of consulting you're doing, it would be difficult to estimate the time required for this business. To be in

control of your schedule, just accept, postpone, and decline jobs based on your desired work schedule.

Estimated Income:
Your income will depend on the demand for your services. Your rates will vary depending on the type of consulting you offer and the going rate in the area of the country in which you live. Check around for the going rate for your chosen type of consulting in your area, and offer a competitive rate.

Estimated Investment Needed:
The investment needed will depend on the type of consulting you offer. You may or may not need formal training and/or licensing. You'll need to research any possible requirements for the area of consulting in which you're choosing to work.

Advertising:
I highly recommend placing and ad in your telephone book. Depending on the type of consulting you're offering, you could leave business cards at various places that may attract potential clients. Word of mouth would be great advertising, too.
If you're offering some type of business consulting, you could send letters offering your services to relevant locations.
You could also set up a website and advertise online.

Additional Information and Resources:
The following resources may offer helpful information for your consulting business.
- www.en.wikipedia.org/wiki/Consultant
- www.unixwiz.net/techtips/be-consultant.html
- Getting Started in Consulting by Alan Weiss
- The Consultant's Quick Start Guide: An Action Plan for Your First Year in Business by Elaine Biech
- Consulting For Dummies by Bob Nelson and Peter Economy
- Flawless Consulting: A Guide to Getting Your Expertise Used by Peter Block

Custom Cake Baking & Decorating

What You'll Do:

As a professional cake baker and decorator, you'll design, bake, and decorate made-to-order cakes for special occasions based on your customers' input and desires. You may create specialty cakes for weddings, birthday parties, anniversaries, engagements, graduations, family reunions, and any other occasion people deem to be special.

You'll offer your customers different options for sizes, flavors, and designs. You can create a portfolio with pictures of cakes you've made so customers will have designs to choose from. You could also let them sketch their own design, or you could sketch a design for them to see if you understand their desired cake.

You may make sheet cakes, tiered cakes, and round cakes. If you really want to specialize, you could even offer ice cream cakes. Just make sure you've got enough freezer space for them.

Once you and your customers decide on the flavor, size, and design, you'll create the cake for the event. You could either offer to deliver it, or you could have your customers pick up the cakes themselves.

What to do with Your Children:

Young children usually like to help out in the kitchen, so you may be able to keep them entertained by letting them stir batter and frosting. Letting them help will almost certainly slow you down and create a bigger mess, but at least you'll get to spend time with them!

You can do the decorating or any intricate details on the cakes while your children are napping, at school, at sports practice, at a playdate, watching a favorite television show, or are being supervised by your husband, a babysitter, or another relative. Just make sure that the children don't stick a finger in the frosting for a taste when they get home!

Estimated Time Required:

You'll most likely spend hours on a single cake. You'll need to mix the batter, bake it, let it cool, frost it, and decorate it. You could easily spend 4 hours on a birthday cake or 8 hours on a wedding cake. The time you devote to this business will depend on the number of cakes you're making per week, the size of the cakes and your oven, and the intricacy of the details and decorations. Your hours will vary.

Estimated Income:

The going rate for cakes will vary depending on the type of cake, the size of the cake, the intricacy of the details, and the going rate in the area of the country in which you live. Contact a local bakery to see what they charge, then charge a competitive price.

Although prices will vary, if it costs you $50 to make a wedding cake, and you sell two wedding cakes each month for $250 each, you'll net $400 per month.

Estimated Investment Needed:

You will need to purchase ingredients to make and decorate the cakes. You'll be responsible for the increased gas or electric bill from the oven to bake the cakes.

If you don't already have enough mixing bowls, kitchen utensils, and other necessary kitchen items, you'll have to buy those, too.

If any licenses, permits, or other regulatory standards are needed, you will also be responsible for those fees.

Advertising:

You could leave brochures and business cards at wedding planners' offices, flower shops, party supply stores, and bridal shops. You could place an ad in the telephone book. You could create a website on which to showcase the cakes you've made. Word of mouth would be great, too.

Additional Information and Resources:

Check with your local government authority to find out the rules and regulations regarding food sales and home baking businesses in your area. Your kitchen may need to be inspected to make sure it's a sanitary environment. You may need a license or permit, and you may need to register your business.

Data Entry

What You'll Do:

As a data entry clerk, you'll type written or printed information, or information on PDF files, into a computer. You may also review scanned information on the computer for accuracy and correct any errors in it or add missing information. When entering the data, you may type the information verbatim, or you may need to type it using numerical codes. You may enter financial information, purchase order numbers, addresses, or other information.

The employment may be temporary or long-term.

What to do with Your Children:

Since this is an online job, you could work from home anytime you have free time. You could work while your children are napping, in bed at night, at school, at sports practice, at a playdate, or even watching television, reading, or playing a game.

Searching online for data entry jobs could be done anytime you're able to use the computer.

Estimated Time Required:

The time required will depend on the number of clients you have, the amount of data that needs entered, and the speed at which you are at entering the data into the computer. There's no reliable estimate for the time required, but it should only be full-time if you want it to be. Just accept and decline jobs based on the amount of time you want to spend working.

Estimated Income:

At the time of this writing, the average income for data entry jobs was in the ballpark of $15 per hour. Pay rates vary in different parts of the country though. If you had 4 jobs per month that each required you to work 16 hours, at a rate of $15 per hour, you'd earn $960 per month. That's just an example though. Your income will depend on your pay rate, the number of data entry projects you do, and the number of hours you spend entering the data.

Estimated Investment Needed:
You will need a computer, and probably internet access.

Advertising:
You could send letters explaining your services to various companies that may outsource their data entry jobs. You could also set up a website if you'd like, and register it with online search engines.
To start out though, I recommend searching for jobs online.

Additional Information and Resources:
Some websites that you may find helpful are listed below.
- www.ELance.com
- www.ScriptLance.com
- www.HireMyMom.com
- www.workathomenoscams.com/work-from-home-companies

Dating Coaching

What You'll Do:
As a dating coach, your job will be to help your clients improve their success in the world of dating. You'll direct your clients on aspects of dating such as how to meet potential partners, how to attract potential partners, and how to determine potential compatibility with prospective dates. You may focus on their wardrobe, their style of flirting, their body language, and other areas that may help them attract a potential mate. You'll try to help them achieve their goals by instructing them, directing them, and offering motivational support. It is coaching. It is not therapy. You'll offer your opinion, words of encouragement, suggestions, or some other type of feedback appropriate for the situation.

You'll provide one-on-one sessions with your clients either over the telephone or in person. You could charge per session or offer a certain number of sessions per week or month and charge a weekly or monthly fee.

What to do with Your Children:
Since your clients both desire and deserve your undivided attention and discretion, your children should not accompany you to one-on-one sessions. They also should not be heard in the background during telephone sessions. You may need to accommodate various schedules for your clients, but you could try to do most of your coaching while your children are in school, at a playdate, at sports practice, or napping. You could also have your husband, a babysitter, or another relative supervise your children for you while you work. If your children are adolescents, they should be able to read a book, watch television, or do some other solo activity while you are in another room conducting a telephone session.

Estimated Time Required:
Coaching sessions will probably last 30 minutes, 45 minutes, or one hour, depending on how long you decide to conduct them.

You could even offer 10 or 15-minute mini telephone sessions for clients who just need a quick motivational boost every day or so.

The time you spend coaching will depend on the number of clients you have and the amount of coaching they desire. Just as an example, if you have only 3 clients who desire two 30-minute sessions per week, that would only be three hours per week.

Decide how much time you want to spend working, and offer sessions of appropriate lengths based on that.

Estimated Income:

At the time of this writing, you could probably earn around $75-125 per hour, depending on the going rate for coaching in your area of the country. You may even charge as little as $25 per hour to get started. Your income would be difficult to estimate beforehand without knowing the demand for the service. Just as an example, if you have just 3 clients and charge them each only $120 per month for a weekly 30-minute session, you'll work 6 hours per month and earn a monthly income of $360. That would be $60 per hour. Of course that's just a very conservative example though. Your income will vary.

Estimated Investment Needed:

There may or may not be a mandatory investment, but you may want to check into insurance in case you were to be sued by an unhappy client who blames you for an unsuccessful relationship.

You could also invest in dating coach training. That could probably range from a few hundred dollars to many thousands of dollars.

Other than that, you'll need a telephone for phone sessions. If you're conducting face-to-face sessions, you'll probably need an office, or you could meet your clients at a restaurant, park, or some other comfortable location.

Advertising:

I highly recommend placing and ad in your telephone book. Since coaching can be done over the telephone, you could also create a website and register your business on online search engines to reach potential clients hundreds and even thousands of miles away. You could also leave business cards at bars and clubs.

Additional Information and Resources:
You can find more information at www.DatingCoach.org.

Daycare Provider

What You'll Do:

As a daycare provider, you'll be responsible for caring for other people's children either in your home or in a building designated as your daycare center. You'll be responsible for all aspects of childcare, including but not limited to keeping them safe, feeding them, changing diapers, cleaning up after them, and putting them down for naps, if necessary.

Most daycare centers are open Monday through Friday from early morning until late afternoon or early evening. You'll set your own hours. Most people who leave their children at daycare centers are working parents, so be sure to make your business hours conducive to working parents' schedules.

If you have a lot of business, you may need to hire help, and you'll most likely need a license and clearances. You'll need to be certified in CPR and first aid, as well.

What to do with Your Children:

If your daycare business is at your home, your children can stay at home with you and play with the other children. If your business is not in your home, bring your children with you to the daycare facility that you're operating.

Estimated Time Required:

Generally, daycare centers are open full-time, so expect at least a 40-hour work week. If you're daycare is open Monday through Friday from 7am to 5pm, that'll be 50 hours. However, if you hire help, you can work however many hours you want.

Estimated Income:

Daycare rates vary greatly in different areas. Check around for rates in your area, and make your rates competitive.

As an example, if you cared for 10 children per day, 5 days per week, at a rate of $30 per day per child, and paid two employees each $8 per hour for 40 hours per week, you'd earn $860 per week, for a total of $3,440 per month, without taking into account any additional expenses. That's just an example though. Your income will vary.

Estimated Investment Needed:
You'll need to obtain any licenses and clearances needed, and CPR and first aid certification. If you're renting a building, you'll be responsible for the cost of the rent. You'll also be responsible for the cost of utilities. If you purchase any toys or gear for your business, you'll have to pay for it but might be able to use it as a tax deduction. You'll also need to pay your employees their wages, if you hire any.

Advertising:
Tell your friends and neighbors since they may have children that need a daycare provider and may be able to recommend you to others. You could hang flyers on public bulletin boards in gyms, libraries, toy stores, grocery stores, and other places that parents may frequent. You could also try radio advertising, newspaper advertising, and taking out an ad in the yellow pages.
The best advertising would probably just be the big sign outside of your business that would state the name of your daycare center and the telephone number.

Additional Information and Resources:
You may want to consider getting references, and of course, be sure your business is properly childproofed.

Delivery Driver

What You'll Do:

To work as a private delivery driver, you'll need to contract with businesses to deliver their products for them. Flower shops may be your best bet for that. If they don't already have someone to deliver their flowers for them, you could ask if they'd be interested in increasing sales by offering delivery services provided by you. You could also contract with bakeries, candy stores, and other businesses as an independent delivery driver.

You'll probably either charge a fixed rate price, or you'll charge by mileage. You could offer to deliver at one certain time every day, or you could offer your services on a few set days per week. Business may be slow at first, but as more and more busy people learn that they can have their purchases delivered for them, business should increase.

What to do with Your Children:

You could work while your children are at school or while your husband or a babysitter is caring for them. You could also work while they are at sports practice or at a playdate.

Estimated Time Required:

The amount of time this business will require of you will depend on the demand for your services and the distance you'll have to travel to make the deliveries.

Estimated Income:

Your income will depend on the number of deliveries you make and the amount you charge. Without knowing those factors, there is no reliable estimate, but just as an example, if you make 3 deliveries per week and charge $15 for each one, you could gross $180 per month. Your earnings will probably fluctuate though, with holidays bringing more business.

Estimated Investment Needed:
You would need an insured vehicle for the deliveries. You'd also need to pay for the fuel, maintenance, and any repairs for the vehicle.

Advertising:
You probably won't advertise for this business. Instead, you'll send letters or approach business owners in person to offer your services.

Additional Information and Resources:
Don't forget to check with your insurance company to see if your policy covers the use of your vehicle for business purposes.

Direct Sales

What You'll Do:
Direct selling is basically the process of sellers selling directly to customers without the customers having to go to retail locations. I can be done by hosting at-home parties, demonstrations, distributing catalogs, or by bringing products directly to the customer for the customer to purchase.

There are many, many companies that offer direct sales positions. Generally, you work as an independent sales representative and earn commissions on your sales. With all of the companies out there, if you do some research, you should be able to find at least one that offers products and commissions that appeal to you. Some may require a start-up fee, but there are many that don't.

To boost your income, you could probably sell products from multiple companies. For example, you could sell both books and cosmetics or cleaning products and candles. You probably wouldn't do a simultaneous demonstration for them, but you could have separate demonstrations or parties or distribute catalogs for both product lines.

What to do with Your Children:
This will depend on what you're selling and how you're selling it. If you're hosting at-home parties or demonstrations, you'll need to leave your children at home when the parties are at another person's house. If you're hosting at your own home, you could have your children supervised by your spouse in the family room or on another floor of the house, you could have your husband take them for a walk, to the park, shopping, or out to dinner, or you could send them to a relative's house.

If you're selling door-to-door, you probably shouldn't bring your children with you. If you're delivering products or catalogs, your children could walk with you, or they could ride with you in the car if you'd like.

Estimated Time Required:
The time you'd devote to this business would depend on the method of selling that you'd use. Parties and demonstrations would likely take around 2 hours each. The time you'd spend delivering products would depend on the number of products that you sell and the distances you'd have to travel to deliver them to your customers. There's not really any reliable way to estimate the time required for direct sales without knowing the method you're using to sell.

Estimated Income:
Your income will depend on the number of sales that you make, the price of the products you sell, and your commission percentages. There is no way to estimate your income without knowing those factors. The company whose products you choose to sell will most likely be able to give you that information.

If you'd like to boost your income, you could probably sell products from more than one company at a time.

Estimated Investment Needed:
You may or may not need to purchase a start-up kit, depending on the product line that you choose to sell. The prices for product kits will vary by business. If you don't want to invest in a start-up kit, there are many companies that don't require you to purchase one. Other than that, you probably won't need any other investment.

Advertising:
You could distribute catalogs, hang flyers, distribute business cards, place an ad in the newspaper, and rely on word of mouth to advertise your direct sales business. The locations at which you advertise would depend on the type of products you're selling.

Additional Information and Resources:
Some websites that you may find helpful for direct sales are listed below.
- www.dsa.org
- www.wfdsa.org

Although I don't endorse any direct sales company, I've listed some websites of direct sales companies for you below to serve as an example.

- www.avon.com
- www.celebratinghome.com
- www.MaryKay.com
- www.pamperedchef.com
- www.tupperware.com
- www.fuller.com
- www.iseeme.com

Dog Obedience Training

What You'll Do:

As an obedience trainer, you'll teach dogs to obey commands. You may teach them to sit, stay, roll over, speak, attack, and/or many others. You may also teach them to quit chewing on shoes and performing other bothersome or destructive habits.

You could conduct one-on-one training with each dog, or you could teach training classes that include multiple dogs with their owners.

The methods you use for training will depend on what you and the dog's owner are comfortable using as teaching methods.

What to do with Your Children:

You'll need to either work while your children are at school, at sports practice, or on a playdate, or you'll need to arrange for childcare for them. Since any animal, especially an untrained animal, could be potentially dangerous, I strongly suggest that you leave your children with your husband, a babysitter, or another relative or friend while you're training the dogs.

Estimated Time Required:

The time you spend working will depend on the method you use for training, one-on-one sessions or group training sessions. You can choose how many sessions you teach per week, so you can pretty much pick the time you'll spend working. Of course you'll only work as many sessions as you have customers for though.

Just as an example, if you teach 5 training sessions per week for 1 hour each, that's only about 20 hours of work per month. If that's too much, you could drop it down to 3 sessions per week. If it's too little, you could teach 2 or 3 sessions per day. Just find what works for you, and stick with that.

Estimated Income:

Your income will depend on the number dogs you'll be training. The going rate for obedience training will vary depending on the area of the country in which you live and the demand for your services. You could probably expect to earn anywhere from $20 to $100 per hour, though you may want to sell the training classes in packages of 5 classes per week for 6 weeks, or some similar package deal.

Estimated Investment Needed:
You'll almost definitely want to look into training for this profession. The owners of the dogs will provide leashes, shock collars, or any other training device you specify that the dogs will need for training. You may need to provide dog treats though.

Advertising:
You could place an ad in the newspaper and telephone book. You could hang flyers and leave business cards at veterinarians' offices, pet stores, and animal rescue shelters. You could also hang flyers on public bulletin boards in malls that have pet stores.

Additional Information and Resources:
Don't forget to check into requirements and laws in your state regarding dog training.
Some websites that may be helpful to you for your dog training business are listed below.
- www.playfulpups.com
- www.ccpdt.org
- www.dogproblems.com
- www.apdt.com

Dog Walking

What You'll Do:

As a dog walker, you'll pick the dogs up from their owners, generally at the same time every day, for a specified amount of time, usually an hour. You'll take them for a daily or twice-daily walk to allow them to get exercise and fresh air, and to relieve themselves. You'll clean up their waste, and properly dispose of it. You may need to water the dogs on hot days, too. Then, you'll return them to their owners.

If you and the dog owners are comfortable with you walking multiple dogs at a time, you may walk dogs for multiple clients at the same time, thus saving you time or freeing up more of your time for additional clients.

What to do with Your Children:

Children generally like animals, so as long as you and your clients are comfortable with it, and there are no potentially dangerous dogs, you may bring your children along with you. Just make sure to properly educate them on animal care and safety.

If your children are older, you could walk the dogs while they're in school, and bring them along on the weekends and during summer break.

Estimated Time Required:

You will generally walk the dogs in 1-hour sessions either every day of the week or every day that their owners are at work and unable to do it themselves. The number of clients you accept will determine the amount of time you spend working. The number of dogs you walk at a time will also be a factor. You can decide how much time you'd like to spend walking dogs, and expand or limit your client base to match your ideal amount of hours.

Estimated Income:
Dog walkers charge different amounts in different parts of the country. Ask around for the going rate in your area, and charge accordingly. The less you charge, the more clients you'll have, but don't forget to decide how much your time is worth to you.

Estimated Investment Needed:
There is probably no mandatory investment for this business. You might want to invest in some comfortable walking shoes, sunblock, and a pooper scooper or latex gloves and plastic bags.

Advertising:
Hanging flyers on telephone poles in your area should attract the attention of people who walk their dogs themselves, and maybe they'll consider giving you a try or recommending you to a friend. Newspaper advertising could also be helpful.

You could also place an ad in the telephone book and hang flyers at pet stores, animal shelters, and veterinarians' offices.

Additional Information and Resources:
If you have any questions or concerns about animal care, feel free to contact your local humane society or animal shelter.

Check with your local government authority for the specifics on leash laws and pooper scooper laws in you're your area.

Editing

What You'll Do:
As an editor, you'll edit printed media. You may edit books, magazine articles, or some other type of written work. You may correct spelling, grammar, and other problems within the written works.

For this job, you'll need to have a firm grasp of your language, with knowledge of proper grammar, spelling, verb tenses, adjective uses, and other proper word uses, punctuation, and formats.

What to do with Your Children:
Since your job hinges on complete accuracy, you might want to work while your children are napping, at school, or being supervised by your spouse. If you need a large block of time to work, you could hire a babysitter if necessary.

Estimated Time Required:
The time you'd spend working would depend on the length of the written works you'd be editing, the number of errors you'd be correcting, and how quickly you could proofread and edit the written works. Without knowing those factors, there is no reliable estimate for the amount of time you'd spend working. Just accept jobs based on the amount of time you want to spend working.

Estimated Income:
There is no reliable estimate of income for this job. Pay rates vary greatly by project.

Estimated Investment Needed:
You would need a computer. A dictionary and thesaurus may be helpful, but there are free dictionary and thesaurus websites that you could use.

Advertising:

You could place an ad in the telephone book and create a website if you'd like. To start out, you could search for jobs online.

Additional Information and Resources:

The following resources may be helpful for this income stream.
- www.ELance.com
- www.scriptlance.com
- www.dictionary.com
- www.thesaurus.com
- www.fabjob.com/BookEditor.asp
- www.en.wikipedia.org/wiki/Editor
- Copyediting & Proofreading For Dummies by Suzanne Gilad
- The Copyeditor's Handbook: A Guide for Book Publishing and Corporate Communications by Amy Einsohn
- Developmental Editing: A Handbook for Freelancers, Authors, and Publishers by Scott Norton
- McGraw-Hill's Proofreading Handbook by Laura Killen Anderson

Fact Checking

What You'll Do:
As a fact checker, you'll basically be conducting research. You'll research the correctness of statements, numerical figures, and other information presented as being factual. You'll generally be given a short deadline for verifying the accuracy of the information. Most of the information you confirm as being factual will probably be used in print in articles or advertisements.

To conduct your fact-checking, you could use various sources for your information. You could search online. You could look in a book. You may even need to collect information via the telephone. It would depend on the information that you need to research. Just make sure to cite the source of the information.

What to do with Your Children:
You could work from home anytime you have free time from which you won't be distracted. You could work while your children are napping, in bed at night, at school, at sports practice, or at a playdate. Just make sure that you only accept jobs that you'll be able to complete by the deadline stated.

Estimated Time Required:
The time required for this business would depend on the number of clients you have and how quickly you can research the information. There's no reliable estimate for the time required, but it probably wouldn't be full-time. Just accept and decline jobs based on the amount of time you have available for research.

Estimated Income:
At the time of this writing, you could probably earn between $15 and $25 per hour. If you were a political fact checker, you could probably earn more. Pay rates vary in different parts of the country. If you worked 2 hours per day, 5 days per week, at a rate of $20 per hour, you'd earn $800 per month. That's just an example though.

Your income will depend on your pay rate, the number of fact-checking jobs you have, and the number of hours you spend on research.

Estimated Investment Needed:
You will probably need a computer and internet access.

Advertising:
You could email letters explaining your services to various companies that may outsource their fact-checking jobs. You could also set up a website and register it with online search engines.
To start out though, I recommend searching for jobs online.

Additional Information and Resources:
Some websites that you may find helpful are listed below.
- www.ELance.com
- www.ifreelance.com
- www.ScriptLance.com
- www.HireMyMom.com
- www.workathomenoscams.com/work-from-home-companies

Fitness Instruction

What You'll Do:
    As a fitness instructor, you'd conduct classes in exercise routines for which you're qualified to teach. It could be aerobics, water aerobics, pilates, or even yoga. If you're not certified in any type of fitness instruction, you probably could be in as little as a few days. When I checked in to it a few years ago, there was a class that lasted only 2 days that, upon completion, would certify you to be an aerobics instructor.
    Of course you'll need a location at which to conduct your classes, too. You could rent a rental hall or see if your local gym would let you use an area of their facility to conduct your classes. Of course you'd pay them a fee for that. If you'll be working as a personal trainer, you'll probably just go to your clients' homes or meet them at a gym.
    Once you've got a place to conduct the classes, you'll decide on the days and times you'll be conducting the classes. Post the days and times on a flyer at the place you're conducting classes and anywhere you wish to advertise.
    You can charge a per-class fee, or you could charge a monthly fee for unlimited classes.

What to do with Your Children:
    You could set your work hours to be when your children are at school or sports practice. You could work when your spouse is home to stay with them. You could also hire a babysitter or have another relative care for them.

Estimated Time Required:
    Exercise classes are generally 1-hour sessions, but may be as short as half an hour. You'll decide when to conduct the classes, but I would recommend 3 evening classes and at least 3 morning classes per week. You may want to add a few afternoon classes, too, but that's up to you.

If you conduct 1-hour classes and have a morning class 5 days per week, 3 evening classes per week, and just 1 afternoon class per week, you'd only be working 9 hours per week.

Estimated Income:

Your income will vary depending on the going rate in your area and the number of people in your classes. As an example, if you charge each person $5 per class and have 10 people attend a class 3 times per week, you'll earn $600 per month before any expenses. You may charge more or less, but that gives you an idea.

Estimated Investment Needed:

If you're not already certified to teach an exercise class, you'll need to pay to become certified. You may be able to do that for around $600 depending on where you get certified and what you get certified for. It could easily cost more, though, so shop around.

You'll need to pay rent at the facility you're renting to conduct your classes. If you're using a gym, you may be able to offer them a percentage of the money you earn from each class. You'll have to try to negotiate that. If you'll be working as a personal trainer, you'll probably just go to your clients' homes or meet them at a gym.

Advertising:

Hang flyers at gyms, grocery stores, and even restaurants. You could also place an ad in the newspaper.

Additional Information and Resources:

You'll need to check with the facility at which you're conducting your classes to see if your class will be covered under their insurance policy or if you'll need to purchase your own insurance.

Check with the fitness director at your local college or university for recommendations on where to get certified to be a fitness instructor. They may even host a class that you could attend to become certified, and it would probably be your least expensive option.

Flipping Houses

What You'll Do:

Flipping houses is a form of real estate investing. You'll find a property that catches your eye. It could be a property that is owned by an individual or a foreclosure owned by a bank. You'll tour the property, and you'll probably bring a contractor along with you. The contractor could probably tell you what needs fixed and how much it would cost to make the repairs and improvements. You'll probably use that information to offer the seller less than the asking price and try to bargain for a good deal.

To purchase the house and pay for the improvements, you could apply for a mortgage, use a home equity line of credit, or take out some other type of loan. Once you own the house, you'll have the repairs and improvements made. Then, you'll put the house up for sale with an asking price of more that you paid to purchase and repair it.

After you buy the house, your goal will be to have it repaired and sold again as soon as possible to limit the amount of time you'll be responsible for the utility bills and property taxes. Once you re-sell the house, you should be able to pay off the loan in full, with the excess money being your profit.

What to do with Your Children:

Anytime you have free time, you could search online for potential houses to buy. You could tour the houses while your children are at school or being supervised by someone else. If you had to, you could bring your children with you when you tour the properties.

You won't need to be present for the repairs, and if you list the property with a realtor, the realtor will show it to potential buyers for you, so your time with your children won't be affected much with this income stream unless you're doing the improvements yourself.

Estimated Time Required:
The time you spend on this income stream will depend on the location of the houses you're touring and whether you're completing any repairs yourself or hiring a contractor for the entire project. If you're only searching for houses and touring them, the time you spend working will be extremely minimal. Your contractor and realtor will do most of the work for you.

Estimated Income:
The amount of income you earn will depend on the purchase price of the house, the cost of the repairs, and the amount for which you re-sell it.

Just as an example, if you purchase a foreclosure for $35,000, pay $15,000 for repairs, pay a realtor 6% of the sale price, and sell the house for $65,000, you'll pocket $14,100 before figuring in costs from the loan, taxes, utilities, insurance, and closing costs. That is just an example though. Your income will vary.

Estimated Investment Needed:
You'll need to pay for the house, the closing costs, the repairs, the taxes, the insurance, and the utilities. You'll probably take out a loan to cover those costs and pay it off as soon as you sell the house.

Advertising:
You probably won't necessarily advertise that you flip houses. You'll just list the repaired houses with realtors and let them advertise the houses for sale for you.

Additional Information and Resources:
Don't forget to check with your local government authority for laws, rules, and regulations, and for possible building permits you may need. You could also inquire about any applicable taxes.

The following resources may contain information that could be helpful for this income stream.
- www.Realtor.com
- www.Owners.com
- www.ForSaleByOwner.com
- FLIP: How to Find, Fix, and Sell Houses for Profit by Rick Villani, Clay Davis, and Gary Keller

- Flipping Houses For Dummies by Ralph R. Roberts and Joe Kraynak
- Flipping Confidential: The Secrets of Renovating Property for Profit In Any Market by Kirsten Kemp
- Fast Real Estate Profits in Any Market: The Art of Flipping Properties--Insider Secrets from the Experts Who Do It Every Day by Sebastian Howell
- Find It, Fix It, Flip It!: Make Millions in Real Estate--One House at a Time by Michael Corbett
- Foreclosure Investing For Dummies by Ralph R. Roberts and Joe Kraynak
- The Complete Guide to Flipping Properties by Steve Berges

Florist

What You'll Do:
As a florist, you'll sell flowers and make and sell flower arrangements. You'll need to have either a separate building for your flower shop, or you'll need a room in your house that is large enough to devote to your business and can be entered into directly from outside.

You'll need to have an inventory for this business, and the bulk of your inventory will be perishable. You may or may not want to offer delivery services.

You'll probably have pre-made arrangements on display for sale, and you'll offer custom arrangements as well. You may sell a single rose, a bouquet of tulips, or an arrangement of assorted flowers. It will depend on your customers' tastes and budget.

To save yourself some money on wasted inventory, you could offer both live flowers and nonperishable silk floral arrangements.

What to do with Your Children:
You could work while your children are at school or while your husband or a babysitter is caring for them. If the flower shop is in your home, you could just have a device on the door to alert you when a customer enters and only leave the door unlocked during set business hours. If you're doing that, your children may be with you in the business. After all, they live there too, and as long as your customers are satisfied with their purchase, it shouldn't matter to them if your children are present.

Estimated Time Required:
The amount of time this business will require of you will depend on the demand for flowers, whether or not you offer deliveries, and the amount of time you want to devote to working. If the business is in your home, aside from making the floral

arrangements, you could have your business open for many hours per day but only have to go into the shop when customers come.

Estimated Income:

Your income will depend on the number of sales you make, your prices, and the amount of perishable inventory that isn't used before it goes bad. Without knowing those factors, there is no reliable estimate of income for this business. Some months will be busier than others. The bulk of your sales will probably be around holidays and in warmer months when most weddings occur.

Estimated Investment Needed:

You would need a location in which to operate your business and all of the necessary insurance, permits, and/or licenses for it. You would need an inventory. Your inventory would probably consist of various types of flowers, vases, baskets, tissue paper, cards, ribbon, and other such items. You'll also need containers or buckets of water and coolers in which to keep the flowers.

Advertising:

You could place an ad in the telephone book and newspaper. You could also hang flyers or leave business cards at party supply stores, jewelry stores, candy stores, bakeries, bridal shops, and other businesses. Of course you'd put a sign in front of your flower shop, and that may be the best method of advertising.

Additional Information and Resources:

Don't forget to check with your local government authority to see what permits
are needed for your business. Most likely, you'll need to register your business, too.

You may find some of the following resources helpful for this business.
- FabJob Guide to Become a Florist by Alisa Gordaneer
- How to Open & Operate a Financially Successful Florist and Floral Business Both Online and Off: With Companion CD - ROM by Stephanie N. Beener
- Start Your Own Florist Shop and Other Floral Businesses by Cheryl Kimball

Flyer Distribution Services

What You'll Do:

Flyer distribution is a marketing technique. You could hand out flyers for multiple businesses at the same time with ads on the same flyer or with individual flyers, or you could hand out flyers for one sole business at a time which would increase the effectiveness of the marketing.

You could hand out flyers door-to-door, at a mall or other business, or you could pay to have them inserted in a newspaper, such as is done with many sale papers. You could also put them on car windshields.

To have a flyer distribution service, you'll offer your service to businesses by explaining the benefits of it. Since flyer distribution is usually less expensive than direct mailing, you should be able to acquire clients rather quickly.

The businesses may provide you with a flyer of which you'll have to reproduce yourself, or they may provide the total number of flyers for you to distribute. If you need to make the copies yourself, you'll charge a bit more for your services to cover the cost of the copies.

What to do with Your Children:

You'll appear more professional if your children don't accompany you while you meet with potential clients. You could meet with clients when your children are at school, being cared for by your spouse, or being watched by a babysitter. You could also make any necessary telephone calls at those times or when your children are napping.

If you're distributing the flyers door-to-door, you should not bring your children with you if you'll be knocking on the doors. If you'll just be leaving the flyers in the doors without having contact with the residents, you could bring your children along for the walk.

If you're having the flyers distributed in newspapers, you could bring your children along with you when you deliver the flyers to the printers' office, or you could go while they're being cared for by someone else or when they're in school.

Estimated Time Required:
There is no reliable estimate of the time required for this business. It will depend on the method of distribution you're using, the number of flyers you're distributing, and the number of clients you have. Decide how much time you want to devote to this business, and accept and postpone distributions based on that figure.
Of course, you could always pay reliable employees to distribute the flyers for you if you don't mind sharing the profits with them.

Estimated Income:
Your income will depend on the price you charge and the number of flyers you distribute. At the time of this writing, 10 cents per flyer would probably be a reasonable price. If you charge 10 cents per flyer distributed, and offer flyer distribution in increments of 1,000, distributing 1 lot of flyers for 1 business per week would earn you $400 per month. If you distributed 5,000 per week at the same rate, you'd earn $2,000 per month. Those are just examples though. If you paid employees to distribute the flyers for you, you'd have to deduct their earnings from those figures.

Estimated Investment Needed:
You probably won't need to put forth an investment for this business. If you're making copies of the flyers to distribute, get a deposit beforehand so the money won't come out of your pocket.

Advertising:
You could call, send letters, or show up in person to businesses for which you'd like to distribute flyers. You could put an ad in the telephone book or newspaper. To advertise and demonstrate your services at the same time, you could hand out flyers!

Additional Information and Resources:
You may be able to find some helpful information for this business on the websites listed below.
- www.articlesnatch.com/topic/flyer+distribution+service

- www.real-business-opportunities.com/category/start-a-flyer-distribution-business
- www.en.wikipedia.org/wiki/Leaflet_distribution

Food Critic

What You'll Do:
    As a food critic, you'll write about various foods and/or restaurants. You'll analyze the foods, noting smells, flavors, textures, appearance, and other relevant information. You'll write articles for publication based on your analyses.
    You could work as a freelance food critic and submit your articles to various media outlets online and in print, you could apply for an existing job as a food critic, or you could contact a media outlet and inquire about the possibility of them printing your articles on a regular basis. There are many websites, magazines, and newspapers that print articles of that nature. You could write a weekly column, a monthly blog, or some other scheduled article frequency.

What to do with Your Children:
    Since you'll need to focus on the task at hand, your children should not accompany you to the restaurants as they may be a distraction. You could try to do most of your tasting while your children are in school, at a playdate, at sports practice, at Sunday school, or napping. You could also have your husband, a babysitter, or another relative supervise your children for you while you're out and/or while you're writing.
    If your children are adolescents, they should be able to read a book, watch television, or do some other solo activity while you are typing, editing, and submitting the review.
    If you're reviewing pre-packaged foods, you could bring your children with you to the grocery store when you purchase those foods.

Estimated Time Required:
    The time you spend at a restaurant will probably last 30 minutes to an hour. If you're critiquing a food you've purchased at a grocery store or as take-out, you would spend time driving to get it and bringing it home to sample it.

The time you spend will depend on how often you'll be writing your articles. A weekly column could take a mere hour or two of your time every week. A daily blog could take up 10 hours per week. Those are just examples though. Your hours will vary.

Estimated Income:
Your income will depend on the frequency of your articles and the pay rate of the media outlets that publish them. There is no reliable estimate of income without knowing that information.

Estimated Investment Needed:
Other than the food you buy, there's probably no mandatory investment, but you could buy a couple books on the subject if you'd like. If you're an employee of a media outlet, they may pay you or reimburse you for your food purchases.

Advertising:
You won't be advertising for this job. Instead, you'll search for jobs online and contact various media outlets to inquire about their potential publication of your articles.

Additional Information and Resources:
The following resources may be helpful to you for this job.
- www.careerbuilder.com
- www.fabjob.com/FoodWriter.asp
- www.weddingwire.com/shared/Rate
- Will Write for Food: The Complete Guide to Writing Cookbooks, Restaurant Reviews, Articles, Memoir, Fiction and More by Dianne Jacob
- Resource Guide for Food Writers by Gary Allen
- Make Money as a Food Writer in Six Lessons by Pamela White

Forex Trading

What You'll Do:

Forex stands for foreign exchange market. Forex trading is trading currencies. It can be very risky, so think it through carefully before making a decision.

Similar to the stock exchange, the foreign exchange market allows you to buy and sell in the hopes of turning a profit. For example, if the euro is valued at less than the dollar, you would buy a quantity of euros. Perhaps then you would be in possession of 110 euros but would have only paid 100 dollars for them. You would then hold the euros until their value rises above that of the dollar. You would then sell the euros for dollars. Perhaps you would be able to buy 120 dollars with the 110 euros you had. That is just an example, and you're not limited to just dollars and euros. You could trade yen, won, pesos, and other currencies.

You can do forex trading at your home computer nearly anytime. The market is open 24 hours a day, except on weekends. If you're willing to take the risk, forex trading could be quite lucrative, but since it can be risky, I highly recommend you research it before jumping in.

What to do with Your Children:

Since the foreign exchange market is open 24 hours a day, except on weekends, you're sure to have your weekends free to spend with your family. You could do your trading while your children are napping, at school, or even when they're asleep for the night or before they get up in the morning. If you'd prefer to do your trading and research during other hours, you could do so while your spouse plays with your children, or you could invite their grandparents or aunt and uncle over to keep them occupied.

If you attempt forex trading, I recommend that you choose a block of time that you'll be completely free of distractions.

Estimated Time Required:
The time you spend working can vary greatly. It's like a waiting game and requires you to be very patient. If you act hastily, it could cost you money. Checking the currency values doesn't take long, but if you check frequently, the time will add up.

You could spend just an hour per week working. You could work ten hours per week. You decide how much time you want to spend researching and checking currency values, but the time involved will probably be minimal.

Estimated Income:
There is no reliable estimate of income for this income stream. You could make a few dollars. You could make hundreds, thousands, or millions of dollars. You could even lose money. To be honest, I'm not sure what percentages of luck and skill are required, but I used a free trial (a practice version) to see if I'd be any good at forex trading, and I just couldn't get the hang of it. Some people get rich from it, others lose money. If you try it, I hope you become one of the people who strike it rich.

Estimated Investment Needed:
You would need a computer with internet access and money to invest. The minimal investment amount would depend on the website through which you chose to make your transactions. Some may require a $10 investment. Some may require $10,000. Choose a website that won't require you to invest more than you're willing to lose.

Advertising:
There is no advertising needed. It's just you and a computer. You'll have no clients or customers. It's pretty much a solo operation.

Additional Information and Resources:
At the time of this writing, the following websites were offering free trials with virtual money or a forex trading simulator, so you'd get to practice before risking any real money.
- www.forex.com
- www.gftforex.com/freetrial/

- www.download3000.com/download_16184.html
- www.FXDD.com
- www.fxcm.com/free-forex-demo

Freelance Copywriting

What You'll Do:

As a copywriter, you'll write advertisements to promote a person, product, business, or idea. The advertisements you write could be used in various forms of media. They could be used as a print ad in a magazine, a catchy jingle on the radio, or even a commercial on television.

The purpose of the words you use will be to persuade the audience to support an idea or person, or to buy a product. They could also be used to dissuade the audience, such as to vote against someone in an election. Either way, your words are to ignite a passion in the audience about the subject.

What to do with Your Children:

Do not bring your children with you when meeting your clients face-to-face. Instead, you could meet with them while your children are at school, sports, or grandma's house. You could also meet with clients at times when your husband would be home to watch your children.

If you're gathering information from a client over the telephone or via email, you can do that in the comfort of your home while your children are napping, playing quietly, or watching television.

You can use any uninterrupted time you have to type up the ads, though coming up with ideas for them could be done anytime. Just make sure you've always got a pen and paper or a voice recorder ready to record your thoughts and ideas. You could type them while your kids are napping, at school, or while your husband is playing with them.

You can fax, email, or deliver the finished copy, depending on the form in which the company or person wishes to receive it, but if you deliver it in person, leave your children at home.

Searching online for copywriting jobs could be done anytime you are able to use the computer.

Estimated Time Required:
The time required will depend on the number of clients you have and how particular they are about their ads. It will also depend on how quickly you think of ideas for the ads. There's no reliable estimate for the time required, but it shouldn't be full-time unless you want it to be. Just accept and decline jobs based on the amount of time you want to spend working.

Estimated Income:
At the time of this writing, a good estimate of income for freelance copywriters is $25-$75 per hour. What you charge will probably depend on the demand for your services, but if you had 3 jobs per month that each required you to work 8 hours, at a rate of $40 per hour, you'd earn $960 per month. That's just an example though. Your income will depend on your rates, the number of clients you have, and the number of hours you spend working on the projects.

Estimated Investment Needed:
There's probably no mandatory investment for this business. You may need a computer and internet access. You'll probably need either pens and paper or a voice recorder. That should be about it.

Advertising:
You could send business cards and letters explaining your services to local businesses, nonprofit organizations, and even to politicians. You could place an ad in the telephone book. You could also set up a website if you'd like, and register it with online search engines.

Additional Information and Resources:
Although you'll probably want potential clients to call you for your services, you may want to try contacting them through online job listing sites. Some websites that you may find helpful for that are listed below.
- www.ELance.com

- www.ScriptLance.com
- www.DailyFreelanceJobs.com
- www.GetAFreelancer.com
- www.FreelanceWriting.com
- www.workathomenoscams.com/work-from-home-companies

Freelance Writing for Periodicals

What You'll Do:
As a freelance writer, you'll write articles, short stories, reviews, poems, jokes, or other works. Then, you'll submit them for publication to magazines, newsletters, and/or other periodicals. You could even write for online magazines and newsletters.

You could query about writing a certain piece and wait for a response before starting the proposed work, or you could write the work and submit the entire manuscript for publication.

You could write general pieces, but you'd probably have better results if you specialized in a specific subject, topic, or area of expertise. You could write about fitness, nutrition, parenting, organizing, gardening, teaching, marriage, dating, religion, politics, or virtually any other genre, fiction or nonfiction.

You'll be paid per article that you sell, but some publications may not pay for unsolicited articles, so make sure to familiarize yourself with the publications before submitting anything to them.

What to do with Your Children:
You could work from home anytime you have free time. You could work while your children are napping, in bed at night, at school, at sports practice, at a playdate, or even watching television or playing a game. If you're writing children's stories or articles, you could sit at the table with your children and get their input while you work.

Estimated Time Required:
The time required will depend on the types of articles you're writing. Articles that require you to perform research will require more time than ones that don't. Poems may require less time than short stories. There's no real estimate for the time required, but

unless you're working with a publisher that has given you a strict deadline, you can spend as much or as little time working as you'd like.

Estimated Income:
Your income will depend on the number of articles that you sell and the amount of money you earn per article. You might earn $20 for a joke, $200 for a short story, $1,000 for an article. Those are just examples though. Your income will vary. Different publications have different pay rates for the works that they purchase. There is no reliable estimate of income for this income stream without knowing those factors.

Estimated Investment Needed:
There's probably no mandatory investment for this business. You should have a computer on which to type your manuscript, and you'll need internet access if you're submitting your works online.

Advertising:
You probably won't advertise that you're writing. Instead, you'll send query letters and/or your manuscript to publishers to see if they'd be interested in publishing your works.

Once your written work is purchased, it'll appear in the periodical that purchased it, so the advertising will be done for you by the company that prints the periodical.

If you'd like to write a regular column or make frequent written contributions in a certain publication, you could inquire with them about the possibility of writing for them on a regular basis.

Additional Information and Resources:
Some resources that you may find helpful are listed below.
- www.WritersMarket.com
- www.rd.com/submitJokePage.do
- www.mothering.com/submission-guidelines
- www.cricketmag.com/pages_content.asp?page_id=22
- www.busyparentsonline.com/Writing/submissionguidelines.htm

- The Best of the Magazine Markets for Writers 2009 by Marni Mcniff
- Magazine Markets for Children's Writers 2010 by Marni E. McNiff
- 2010 Writer's Market Deluxe by Robert Lee Brewer

Gardening and Farming

What You'll Do:

As a gardener or farmer, you'll either grow produce and/or other plants, or you'll raise animals. You could grow a variety of fruits and vegetables to sell, or you could specialize in just one item, such as strawberries, pumpkins, shrubs, or even Christmas trees. You could raise chickens to sell for meat, or you could sell the eggs that they lay. You could raise pigs, ducks, or cows for meat or to sell live to others.

Gardening and farming is a very broad area. You could have a small herb garden and sell what you don't think you'll use. You could have a small vegetable garden and sell the surplus of your harvest. You could have just a few chickens and sell any extra eggs you gather, or you could let them hatch and sell the chicks. If you'd like a larger business, you could include large numbers of animals or fields of produce.

In this business, you're limited by the amount of land you have and the amount of work you're willing to put forth, but you could earn money from any size farm or garden.

In this business, you'll be subject to various government regulations. Be sure to contact your local government authority to find out more about the laws, rules, and regulations that you'll need to follow.

What to do with Your Children:

Young children usually like to help out in the garden and with animals, so you may be able to keep them entertained by letting them help you.

If you don't want them to help you, you could work while your children are napping, at school, at sports practice, at a playdate, or being supervised by your husband, a babysitter, or another relative.

Estimated Time Required:
　　The amount of time required for this business will depend on the size of your farm or garden and whether you're growing plants or raising animals. There is no reliable estimate for the amount of time required without knowing those factors.

Estimated Income:
　　Your income will depend on what you're selling and how much of it you sell. There is no reliable estimate of income without knowing those factors.

Estimated Investment Needed:
　　You will need land, not necessarily a lot of land if you're having a small garden or raising only a few chickens in your back yard though.
　　If you're gardening, you'll need to buy the seeds or plants. You could buy fertilizer, or you could use your own compost. You'll probably need gardening gloves, a watering can or hose, and tools such as shovels, rakes, and hoes.
　　If you're raising animals, you'll need to purchase the animals and provide them with shelter, food and water, and medical care.
　　You'll also need to pay for any necessary permits or licenses required for this business.

Advertising:
　　You could leave business cards or hang flyers at natural food stores. You could put a sign up in your yard. You could even set up a produce stand on your property or at a farmer's market. Word of mouth would be great, too.

Additional Information and Resources:
　　Check with your local government authority to find out the rules and regulations regarding this business.
　　The following books may include information that you may find helpful for this business.
- Christmas Trees for Pleasure and Profit by Robert D. Wray
- Micro Eco-Farming: Prospering from Backyard to Small Acreage in Partnership with the Earth by Barbara Berst Adams

- Organic Farming: Everything You Need to Know by Peter V. Fossel
- Backyard Market Gardening (Good Earth) by Andy, W Lee and Patricia, L Foreman
- Raising Chickens For Dummies by Kimberley Willis and Rob Ludlow
- The Joy of Keeping Chickens: The Ultimate Guide to Raising Poultry for Fun or Profit by Jennifer Megyesi and Geoff Hansen

"Get Paid to Drive" Advertising

What You'll Do:

To work as a driver for a "get paid to drive" company, you'll be paid to drive a vehicle with a large advertisement on it, usually just as you go about your daily routine of running errands. You may be provided with a company car, or you may have a decal advertisement on your own vehicle.

You'll need to do a minimum amount of driving for this job, but the amount of time you spend running errands may be sufficient. Even having the vehicle in the parking lot of a grocery store while you shop is advertising.

Your monthly pay will probably be a fixed amount. It'll be like a rental fee for the company renting space on your vehicle. Your vehicle will be like a mobile billboard.

What to do with Your Children:

The beauty of this job is that, unless you don't drive much already, you won't need to alter your routine at all. If the company for which you're advertising requires you to drive more than you already do, you could just bring your children along for the drive.

Estimated Time Required:

The amount of time this business will require of you will depend on the amount of driving time required by the company for which you're advertising. You may or may not need to drive anymore than you already do. Since the advertisement will be on your vehicle, it'll be like a 24/7 advertisement no matter where you are or what you're doing.

Estimated Income:

Your income will depend on the company for which you're advertising. If you're provided with a company car, you'll probably be paid less than if you're driving your own vehicle. At the time of this writing, you could probably expect to earn anywhere from $200 to $1,000 dollars per month.

Estimated Investment Needed:
If you're driving your own vehicle, you'll of course need a vehicle with adequate insurance. Other than that, you'll need to pay for gas, oil changes, and possibly other maintenance on the vehicle, but the company for which you're advertising may reimburse you for part or all of those expenses.

Advertising:
You probably won't advertise your services for this business, though you could if you'd like. If you did, though, you'd only be able to have one, maybe two, clients per vehicle that you're driving. Even if you put ads on your vehicle and your husband's, that would still only be 2-4 clients at a time.
I recommend searching online for jobs of this nature.

Additional Information and Resources:
The following resources may contain helpful information for this income stream.
- www.finance.yahoo.com/family-home/article/107476/make-money-by-simply-driving-your-car.html
- www.freecarmedia.com

Gift Basket Business

What You'll Do:

As a gift baskets business owner, you'll create gift baskets for profit. There is a multitude of themes you could use for your baskets. You could create fruit baskets, baskets of Valentine's Day candies and flowers, Christmas cookie baskets, baby shower baskets, wedding gift baskets, housewarming gift baskets, anniversary gift baskets, Mother's Day and Father's Day gift baskets, Easter baskets, spa toiletries gift baskets, sports gift baskets, graduation gift baskets, and many other types of gift baskets. The possibilities are endless. You could also offer to deliver them, but it would be easier for you and cheaper for your customers if they delivered the baskets themselves.

Since there are so many different possible baskets for you to make, if you're not specializing in any type, you could create a variety of gift baskets, take a photo of each one, and put the photographs in a portfolio with a list of the contents of each basket and the prices. The portfolio could be used like a catalog for your customers whenever they want to decide on a basket to order from you if they don't want any that you have on hand that are already made up.

What to do with Your Children:

You may or may not want to bring your children with you when you go shopping for the empty baskets, the decorations, and the baskets' contents. If you don't want to bring them, you could leave them with your husband or go while they're in school, on a playdate, or at sports practice.

You could assemble the baskets while your children are home, but if you're afraid that your young children will try to be a little too helpful, you could work while they're napping.

As for having your children around when customers pick up their baskets, as long as your children can behave, there should be no problem. After all, your children do live there. As long as your customers are happy with your work, your children being there shouldn't matter to them.

If you're delivering the gift baskets to the customers or recipients, you could allow your children to ride along with you in the car or join you for a walk to your destination. If you think that would make you appear unprofessional, you could leave your children with your husband while you deliver the baskets, or you could deliver them while your children are at school.

Estimated Time Required:

The time required for this business will depend on the demand for your gift baskets. Of course the more you have to make, the more time you'll need to work. To estimate the time required, you'll need to figure in the amount of time it'll take you to consult with your customers, shop for your supplies, and assemble the gift baskets.

Estimated Income:

Your income will depend on the number of gift baskets you sell and the amount you charge per basket. Just as an example, if you sold 3 baskets per week that each cost $35 to make and sold for $65 each, your monthly income would be $360 without figuring in any applicable taxes. Your income will vary, and so will the cost of you supplies and the amount you charge for your gift baskets.

Estimated Investment Needed:

You will need to purchase your gift basket supplies. You'll need to purchase the baskets, the contents of the baskets, perhaps some tissue paper, ribbons, bows, gift cards, and cellophane. If you're making a portfolio of baskets that can be ordered, you'll need to purchase a portfolio. You'll also need to take photographs of the baskets, so you'll need a camera and prints of your photos.

Advertising:

You could leave business cards at party supply stores, jewelry stores, flower shops, department stores, bridal shops, and bakeries. You could hang flyers on bulletin boards at malls.

You could advertise in the newspaper and telephone book, too.

Word of mouth would be great advertising, especially if it came from a happy customer.

If you're willing to mail your gift baskets, you could create a website to showcase your baskets and allow them to be ordered online.

Additional Information and Resources:

The following resources may contain information that could be helpful to you for this business.
- www.giftbasketbusiness.com
- www.giftbasketbusinessworld.com
- www.basketbizhelp.com
- The Perfect Basket: How to Make a Fabulous Gift Basket for Any Occasion by Diane Phillips
- Start Your Own Gift Basket Business by Cheryl Kimball
- Start and Run a Gift Basket Business (With CD-ROM) by Mardi Foster-Walker
- The Business of Gift Baskets : A Guide for Survival by Cynthia McKay and Carol Doris

Gift Wrapping

What You'll Do:

As a professional gift wrapper, you'll wrap gifts for every occasion. You could wrap them in wrapping paper, put them in gift bags, or even assemble them into gift baskets. You can either pick up the gifts from your clients and return them to them when they are wrapped, or your clients could drop them off at your house and pick them up at a specified time. It would be easier for you if your clients handled the transportation of the gifts, and it would be cheaper for them.

Most likely, you'll supply all of the wrapping and packaging materials, such as wrapping paper, tissue paper, tape, and other necessary items. Your clients can supply any necessary cards that they wish to include with the gifts. Your clients can tell you the occasion that the gift is for, the type of packaging they desire (gift bag, wrapping paper, basket), and any color or design preference they may have. If they're having numerous gifts wrapped at the same time, make sure they give you a list of who gets what gift so you can affix the proper tag on each one. You can either fill out the gift tags, or have your clients do it themselves before the gifts are wrapped. Just make sure they end up on the right gifts!

What to do with Your Children:

Some children may be able to be entertained by watching you wrap gifts. Others may try to be a little too helpful. If you're wrapping gifts in the presence of your children, make sure they don't damage any of the gifts. They may get excited thinking a certain toy is for them when it actually belongs to one of your clients. Children who are old enough to both understand and obey may be included by allowing them to hold the tape for you, help choose bows, and other tasks that don't involve directly handling the gifts themselves.

If your children would never allow you to wrap a gift without them helping you, you'll have to work while they're napping, at school, being entertained by your spouse or other family member, on a play date, at sports practice, or even in bed for the night or before they wake in the morning. If you wanted to, you could hire a babysitter to play with them in another room while you work.

As for having your children around when clients drop off and pick up their gifts, as long as your children can behave, there should be no problem. After all, your children do live there. As long as your clients are happy with your work, your children being there shouldn't matter to them.

Estimated Time Required:

It would probably take around 5 minutes to wrap a gift and decorate it with ribbon and a bow. A gift basket may take 10 minutes. Gift bags may only take 2 minutes. Although those are just estimates, the actual times shouldn't be that far off.

Of course the number of gifts you have to wrap will determine how long you work. The Christmas season will probably be when you'll spend them most time working.

Without knowing the number of gifts you'll be wrapping, there is no reliable estimate of time required for this business.

Estimated Income:

Your income will depend on the number of gifts you wrap and the amount you charge per gift. Gift baskets would be more expensive than using wrapping paper, so adjust your prices accordingly. If you wrapped 12 gifts for $2.50 each, you'd work about one hour, and earn $30, not counting the cost of supplies. That could easily be done around Christmas, Easter, an upcoming wedding, and children's birthday parties. That's just an example though. Your prices and income may vary.

Estimated Investment Needed:

You will need to purchase gift wrapping supplies, such as wrapping paper, tape, tissue paper, scissors, ribbon, bows, gift bags, gift tags, gift boxes, and baskets. You may also need cellophane and bubble wrap.

Your chosen venue of advertising may also incur a fee.

Advertising:

You could leave business cards at party supply stores, toy stores, jewelry stores, flower shops, and department stores that don't offer gift wrapping services. You could hang flyers on bulletin boards at malls.

You could advertise in the newspaper and telephone book, too.

If you really wanted to advertise big, you could put flyers on car windshields in mall parking lots.

Word of mouth would be great advertising, especially if it came from a happy customer.

Additional Information and Resources:

If you plan on wrapping a lot of fragile gifts, you may want to consider purchasing insurance.

Some websites that may be helpful for this business are listed below.

- www.lisasgiftwrappers.com
- www.associatedcontent.com/article/512273/your_complete_guide_to_starting_a_gift.html
- www.ehow.com/how_2309329_start-gift-wrapping-business.html
- www.giab.com/overview.html
- www.mysmallbiz.com/part-time-business/starting-a-gift-wrapping-business.php

Health & Wellness Coaching

What You'll Do:
As a health and wellness coach, your job will be to offer guidance, advice, and feedback to your clients with regard to their overall wellbeing. Some of the issues may include dieting, weight loss, exercise routines, stress reduction, stress management, proper nutrition, meditation, and other health and wellness-related issues.

It is coaching. You will not act as a doctor. You may recommend a doctor or therapist if you deem it necessary or helpful, though. However, if your clients are facing physical health issues, they will most likely already be under the care of a physician.

You'll provide one-on-one sessions with your clients either over the telephone or in person. You could charge per session or offer a certain number of sessions per week or month and charge a weekly or monthly fee.

What to do with Your Children:
Since your clients both desire and deserve your undivided attention and discretion, your children should not accompany you to one-on-one sessions. They also should not be heard in the background during telephone sessions. You may need to accommodate various schedules for your clients, but you could try to do most of your coaching while your children are in school, at a playdate, at sports practice, at Sunday school, or napping. You could also have your husband, a babysitter, or another relative supervise your children for you while you work. If your children are adolescents, they should be able to read a book, watch television, or do some other solo activity while you are in another room conducting a telephone session.

Estimated Time Required:
Coaching sessions will probably last 30 minutes, 45 minutes, or one hour, depending on how long you decide to conduct them.

You could even offer 10 or 15-minute mini telephone sessions for clients who just need a quick motivational boost every day or so.

The time you spend coaching will depend on the number of clients you have and how much coaching they desire. If you have only 3 clients who desire two 30-minute sessions per week, that would only be three hours per week.

Decide how much time you want to spend working, and offer sessions of appropriate lengths based on that.

Estimated Income:

At the time of this writing, you could probably earn around $125 per hour, depending on the going rate for coaching in your area. Some coaches charge up to $300 per hour, but that seems exorbitant to me. You could probably charge each client $200-$400 per month for a weekly 30-minute session, though some coaches charge $300-$600. The amount that you charge will probably depend on the going rate in your area of the country, but if you have just 3 clients and charge them each only $200 per month for a weekly 30-minute session, you'll work 6 hours per month and earn a monthly income of $600. That would be $100 per hour. Of course that's just an example though.

Estimated Investment Needed:

You may want to check into insurance in case you were to be sued by a client who misunderstood your motivation or blamed you for an illness or injury.

You could also invest in health and wellness coach training. That could range from a few hundred dollars to many thousands of dollars. In this area of work, certification and training are important credentials.

Other than that, you'll need a telephone for phone sessions. If you're conducting face-to-face sessions, you'll probably need an office, or you could meet your clients at a restaurant, park, or some other comfortable location.

Advertising:

I highly recommend placing and ad in your telephone book. Since coaching can be done over the telephone, you could also create a website and register your business on online search engines to reach potential clients hundreds and even thousands of miles away.

You could also leave flyers and business cards at grocery stores, gyms, doctors' offices, spas, and rehabilitation centers.

Additional Information and Resources:
You may find the following websites helpful for this business.
- www.wellcoach.com
- www.spencerinstitute.com/corporate-wellness-health-promotion.html
- www.magicjack.com

There are other places that offer training. Shop around for one that fits your budget, your schedule, and your preferred style of learning.

Home Staging

What You'll Do:
　　As a home stager, you'll make homes that are for sale more attractive to potential buyers. You could rearrange furniture, paint walls, remove shrubs, update bathroom fixtures, or do anything else that may make the homes more appealing to prospective buyers. Of course for repairs, you'll most likely hire a contractor to complete the work.
　　You could work for realtors, private sellers, home builders, or real estate investors.
　　Don't forget to take before and after photos of your work to include in your portfolio.

What to do with Your Children:
　　Your children should not accompany you to your clients' homes. You could have your spouse, another relative, or a babysitter watch your children while you work. If your children are older, you could work while they are in school, at a play date, or at sports practice. You don't want to risk having your children break anything.

Estimated Time Required:
　　The time required would depend on the demand for your services, the amount of work that the house needs, and the speed at which you can have the work done. Don't overwhelm yourself with too many jobs though. Just accept, postpone, and decline jobs based on your availability for work.

Estimated Income:
　　There is no reliable estimate for your income. It will depend on the demand for your services and the amount you charge. At the time of this writing, I believe the income for a home stager was anywhere from around $75 to $150 per hour, though it could easily be more or less depending on where you live.

Estimated Investment Needed:
    I highly recommend purchasing insurance for this business. You may or may not need a certification, but you could take a class or buy some books on the subject. Investing in training is usually worthwhile.

Advertising:
    You could also leave business cards at real estate offices or offer your services to real estate agents. You could also advertise in the newspaper and place an ad in the telephone book.

Additional Information and Resources:
    Some resources that you may find helpful for this business are listed below.
- www.squidoo.com/home-staging-business
- www.stagedhomes.com/
- www.en.wikipedia.org/wiki/Home_staging
- www.hgtv.com/curb-appeal-the-block/show/index.html
- How to Open & Operate a Financially Successful Redesign, Redecorating, and Home Staging Business: With Companion CD-ROM by Mary Larsen and Teri B. Clark
- Home Staging For Dummies by Christine Rae and Jan Saunders Maresh
- Become a Home-Stager Today!: No Experience? No Problem! by Karen Kelly sds

Housekeeping

What You'll Do:
As a professional housekeeper, you'll clean your clients' houses. Most clients will probably have you clean for them on a regular basis, but some will only use your services for special occasions, such as around holidays, for spring cleaning, or before having houseguests.

Most likely, all of the cleaning supplies will be provided for you at your clients' residences. If you'd like to specialize in organic housekeeping, all-natural housekeeping, or some other niche, you'll provide your own cleaning supplies, but you'll be able to charge higher rates to make up for it.

When cleaning other people's houses, you'll want to agree upon what your duties are. How often will you be dusting the keepsakes in the curio cabinet? Will you be responsible for cleaning out the litter box? Will you be changing the bed sheets? Those are just a few things to think about.

Your clients may or may not be home when you clean. It's easier if they're not home, but some people may not feel comfortable allowing others in their homes when they're not present.

One more important point in housekeeping is discretion. Keep everything in the house private. Don't tell anyone about expensive electronics that may invite a burglar. Don't gossip about medication bottles you see that may embarrass your client. If the house is dirty, don't embarrass your clients by telling others how unsanitary you found the environment to be. After all, if it were clean, they wouldn't need your services. Your job is just to clean, not to snoop, judge, or gossip. Your clients' lives should remain private.

What to do with Your Children:
Your children should not accompany you to your clients' homes. You could have your spouse, another relative, or a babysitter watch your children while you clean. If your children are older, you could work while they are in school, at a play date, or at sports

practice. You don't want to risk having your children break anything, and if you're charging an hourly rate, it wouldn't be fair to your clients if your pace was slowed by distractions.

Estimated Time Required:

The time required would depend on the size of the house, the speed at which you clean, and what your duties are. You could probably clean a 2-bedroom, 1-bath home in less than four hours. You could estimate how long it might take to clean another's house by how long it takes you to clean your house. After the first time you clean a house, you'll have a good idea of how long it'll take the next time.

Estimated Income:

Your income will depend on the number of clients you have and how long it takes you to clean their homes. You could charge an hourly rate or a set rate based upon the number of rooms in the house. You'll probably never earn less than $10 per hour, and you may receive tips, too.

If you charge $12 per hour and clean 3 houses per week for 4 hours each, you'll earn $144 per week, or $576 per month. That's just an example though. Your income will vary.

Of course the amount you charge will depend on the going rate in your area of the country, but you could probably make a decent income from this no matter where you live.

Estimated Investment Needed:

You may not need any investment for this business. If you specialize, you'll need to buy your own cleaning products. You may or may not want to check into purchasing insurance in case you accidentally break something valuable at a client's house.

Advertising:

Word of mouth will be good advertising. To get started, you could also leave business cards and hang flyers at real estate offices, day care centers, pediatricians' offices, family restaurants, toy stores, gyms, and grocery stores. You could also advertise in the newspaper and place an ad in the telephone book.

Additional Information and Resources:

Some websites that you may find helpful for ordering specialty cleaning products are listed below.
- www.diapers.com
- www.drugstore.com
- www.vitacost.com
- www.amazon.com
- www.babyganics.com

Housesitting

What You'll Do:
　　Sometimes when people housesit, they stay at the house they're watching while the owners are gone and even spend the nights there. Since you have children, you obviously won't be doing that, but you can still housesit. To housesit, you just take over the day-to-day responsibilities of taking care of the house, everything in it, and everything outside of it.
　　Generally, you'll be making it appear as though the residence is occupied and someone is home. You'll take care of the sidewalk, shoveling snow or putting salt down to melt the ice in winter. If the owners have a mailbox at their house or subscribe to a newspaper, you'll bring the mail and newspaper into the house everyday. You'll water their plants, feed their fish, perhaps turn lights on for short periods of time to make it appear as though someone is home, and whatever else the owners request of you.
　　If the owners have dogs or cats, they may leave them at a boarding kennel, hire someone else to feed them and walk them, or leave them in your care as part of your housesitting responsibility. You may have to negotiate pet care.

What to do with Your Children:
　　Since the owners want everything to remain as they left it, it's best not to bring your children with you when you check on the inside of the house. However, since you can come and go from the house you're caring for at any time, you could check on it when your children are at school, leave them with your husband for a bit when he gets home from work, or bring them along for outside care of the house.
　　If your children nap, you could have their father, grandmother, or a neighbor stay with them while you sneak out to fulfill your housesitting responsibilities. If they're old enough to stay alone, you

could leave them at home for the half hour or so that it would take you to care for the house.

Estimated Time Required:
You would need to check on the house everyday that the owners were gone, especially if you need to water their plants, feed and walk their pets, or change the litter box. It may only take you 20 minutes. If you have to shovel snow, it may take an hour, but they may hire someone else for snow removal. You may come and go multiple times in a day to turn lights off and on, depending on the homeowner's wishes.

On average, you could probably spend only 20 minutes to an hour per day caring for the house. Your hours will vary by job though.

Estimated Income:
Your income would depend on your duties. You would be paid more if you had to shovel snow, walk pets, or turn lights off and on multiple times a day. The going rate for housesitting varies greatly depending on the size of the house, the location of the house, the number of days you're housesitting, and the responsibilities you're left with.

You'd probably never earn less than $10 per day for very minimal responsibility, but you may easily be able to earn $150 a week if you're left with more responsibilities.

Estimated Investment Needed:
If you have to drive to the house that you're housesitting, you'll have to pay for the gas in your car. Other than that, you shouldn't have any investment costs.

Advertising:
Most people will only hire people that they know to housesit for them. Word of mouth would be the best advertising for you. Tell your friends. After you've housesat for a few acquaintances, they may recommend your services to people that they know, thus giving you credibility and making you appear trustworthy to strangers.

Additional Information and Resources:
　　　Check out ADT.com or another security website for tips on how to make it appear as though someone's home even when they're not.

Human Intelligence Tasks

What You'll Do:
To earn income by performing human intelligence tasks (HITs), you'll register with a website or various websites that pay you to complete tasks that computers can't easily do. You may take surveys, check the correct spelling of searches, translate articles into other languages, look up and confirm item numbers, choose the appropriate categories for products, or complete some other type of task.

Once you're registered with a website to do HITs, you'll log into your account, search the tasks, select the tasks you want to complete, complete them, and submit your work.

Amazon.com may have the most talked-about HITs available now. Various tasks may have different pay rates, but you should be able to see the rate of pay on Amazon's mechanical turk for each task before you accept it.

What to do with Your Children:
Since this is an online job, you could work from home anytime you have free time. You could work while your children are napping, in bed at night, at school, at sports practice, at a playdate, or even watching television or playing a game.

Depending on the task, if you're able to focus, you could even sit at the computer and work while your children are on your lap.

Estimated Time Required:
The time required will depend on the number of HITs you complete and how long it takes you to complete each one. There's no reliable estimate for the time required since the tasks may vary. Just complete tasks for as long and as often as you feel like working.

Estimated Income:

Your income will depend on the number of HITs you complete and the amount of money you earn per HIT. Some HITs may pay a few cents. Some may pay several dollars. It will vary. If, for example though, if you complete one $4 task per day, you'd earn $28 per week, or around $112 per month. That's just an example though. Your income will vary.

Estimated Investment Needed:
You will need a computer and internet access, but if you don't have that, you could go to your local library or some other place that offers free internet access.

Advertising:
You won't advertise for this business. Instead, you'll register with at least one website that pays you to complete HITs.

Additional Information and Resources:
Some websites that you may find helpful for this income stream are listed below.
- www.mturk.com/mturk/welcome
- www.braingle.com/hit.php

Illustrating

What You'll Do:
    As an illustrator, you'll create illustrations, or pictures, for printed material. You'll draw, paint, create digital illustrations, or use some other method to create them. They may be used in books, magazines, greeting cards, advertisements, comics, or other sources.

What to do with Your Children:
    Since you'll want to focus on the illustrations you're creating, you might want to work on them while your children are napping, at school, or being supervised by your spouse. If you need a large block of time to create complex illustrations, you could hire a babysitter if necessary.
    If you won't be distracted, you could have your children sit across the table from you and make their own pictures while you create your illustrations.

Estimated Time Required:
    The time you spend working depends on the number of illustrations you're creating, the complexity of the illustrations, and how quickly you can create each illustration.
    There is no reliable estimate for the amount of time you'll spend working. Just accept jobs based on the amount of time you want to spend working.

Estimated Income:
    There is no reliable estimate of income for this job. Pay rates vary greatly by project.

Estimated Investment Needed:
    You would need whatever art supplies you'll be using to create the illustrations. No formal training is required, but it would probably be helpful.

Advertising:

You could place an ad in the telephone book, send letters and business cards to various publishers, and create a website if you'd like.

To start out, you could search for jobs online.

Additional Information and Resources:

The following resources may be helpful for this income stream.
- www.ELance.com
- www.scriptlance.com
- www.en.wikipedia.org/wiki/Illustrator
- Illustrating Children's Picture Books: Tutorials, Case Studies, Know-How, Inspiration by Steve Withrow and Lesley Breen Withrow

Interior Decorating

What You'll Do:
As an interior decorator, you'll meet with your clients at their homes, offices, or other locations to discuss the styles that they envision. They may want you to Fung Shui their living room, design a jungle-themed nursery, or create a child-friendly atmosphere in their dental clinic.

You can put together a portfolio of styles, designs, furniture, paint samples, fabric swatches, and other relevant materials. After your clients decide what they'd like, you'll probably require a deposit to help with the cost of materials. You may do some or all of the work yourself. You may pay others for reupholstery, architectural, or other services. Just remember to stay within the budget and the timeframe agreed upon.

After you're done, you'll collect the balance of the amount due. You could ask for a letter of recommendation to keep in your portfolio to show to other potential clients.

What to do with Your Children:
Your children should not accompany you when you go to meet with your clients. If you can focus, it shouldn't hurt for you to place the orders for the materials online or over the telephone while your children are at home though.

You could have your spouse, another relative, or a babysitter watch your children while you meet with clients. If your children are older, you could work while they are in school.

Estimated Time Required:
The time required would depend on the size of the project, the timely delivery of materials, and the time it takes for contractors you hire to complete their part of the project. Meeting with clients to discuss their desired styles or themes could take around 2 to 4 hours, depending on how decisive they are.

If a job is too big for you, feel free to decline it and refer the potential client to another interior decorator. This could easily be a full-time job. If you only want to work part-time, accept, decline, and postpone jobs to suit your desired schedule.

Estimated Income:
Your income will depend on the number of clients you have, the size of the jobs, and the styles desired. The amount you charge will depend on the going rate in your area, but you could probably make a decent income from this no matter where you live. The income range for this job fluctuates greatly, but a ballpark figure for around the time of this writing would be around $20 per hour.

Estimated Investment Needed:
You'll need some type of training for this business. Check around for courses in your area or online. Prices will vary. You may or may not need licenses and/or permits. Check your state's requirements to find out.

You'll need money, or at least a credit card, to pay for the materials ordered, unless you charge your clients for them up front. I would recommend charging for them up front, but if you don't charge the entire price, you should at least have them make a small deposit.

I recommend creating a portfolio, but the cost of that should be minimal.

You'll also need transportation to meet with your clients.

Advertising:
Word of mouth will be great advertising for this business. Once you've got one happy client, you can be sure that he or she will tell others about your services.

To get started, you could leave business cards at furniture stores, home improvement stores, and hardware stores. You could also advertise in the newspaper and place an ad in the telephone book.

Additional Information and Resources:
Some resources that you may find helpful are listed below.
- www.wikipedia.org/wiki/Interior_decorator
- FabJob Guide to Become an Interior Decorator by Tag Goulet and Catherine Goulet

- Interior Decorator Business Plan - MS Word/Excel by BizPlanDB, sold on www.Amazon.com
- www.interior-design-school.net/interiordecorator.htm
- www.fabjob.com/Decorator.asp

<u>Interpreting</u>

What You'll Do:
    As an interpreter, your job will be to provide communication for people who speak different languages. You'll be the mediator, or the "go between", for the parties involved. You'll be present for the conversation or presentation that you'll be interpreting.
    You may do sign language for a church service, high school play, corporate presentation, or courtroom witness. You may interpret Spanish, Chinese, or some other language for English-speaking business executives. You could even interpret for doctors and patients at hospitals, clinics, or medical offices. Your services could be needed in any circumstance where there's a language barrier.

What to do with Your Children:
    In most cases, you should not bring your children to work with you for this job. If possible, you could have your husband supervise your children for you while you work, or you may need to leave them with a friend, relative, or babysitter. If you're interpreting at a church, you could bring your whole family with you and allow them to sit in a pew for the service while you're up front. Some companies have on-site daycare centers you could utilize. What you do with your children will depend on where and when you'll be interpreting.

Estimated Time Required:
    The time you spend working will depend on the demand for your services. Your schedule will probably vary. You'll probably work on an as-needed basis.
    To be in control of your schedule, decide how much time you want to spend working, and accept and decline jobs based on that.

Estimated Income:
    At the time of this writing, you could probably earn anywhere from $10 to $30 per hour, depending on your experience and the

going rate for interpreting in your area. Your income would be difficult to estimate beforehand without knowing the demand for your service. If you interpret a weekly church service, at a rate of $18 per hour, you'll work about 4 hours per month, and earn a monthly income of around $72. Of course that's just an example though.

Estimated Investment Needed:
The investment for this job will depend on what languages you currently speak. If English is your only language, you'll need to receive formal training in another language. License and certification requirements vary by state.

Advertising:
You could send business cards and letters explaining your services to churches, schools, corporations, and other businesses. You could call your local government offices to inquire about interpreting for them. You could also place an ad in your local telephone book.

Additional Information and Resources:
The following resources may have information that could be helpful for this job.
- www.360translations.com/burnsat/stateregs.htm
- www.en.wikipedia.org/wiki/Interpreter
- www.pennfoster.edu/spanish
- www.collegegrad.com/careers/proft105.shtml
- Interpretation (Professional Interpreting in the Real World) by James Nolan
- So You Want to Be an Interpreter: An Introduction to Sign Language Interpreting by Jan Humphrey, Bob Alcorn, and Janice H. Humphrey
- Reading Between the Signs: Intercultural Communication for Sign Language Interpreters 2nd Edition by Anna Mindess, Thomas K. Holcomb, Daniel Langholtz, and Priscilla Poynor Moyers
- Sign Language Interpreters in Court: Understanding Best Practices by Carla M. Mathers

- Language into Language: Cultural, Legal and Linguistic Issues for Interpreters and Translators by Saul Sibirsky and Martin C. Taylor
- Deaf Professionals and Designated Interpreters: A New Paradigm by Peter C. Hauser, Karen L. Finch, and Angela B. Hauser
- The Interpreter's Guidebook: Techniques for Programs and Presentations (Interpreter's handbook series) by Kathleen Regnier, Michael Gross, and Ron Zimmerman
- Interpreting at Church: A Paradigm for Sign Language Interpreters, 2nd Edition by Leo Yates

Inventing

What You'll Do:
As an inventor, you'll create new products. You could invent anything you want. Once you've created your invention, you may want to get a patent for it. Then, you'll be ready to market your invention.

You could sell your invention yourself, sell your rights and patent, or use a licensing agreement to allow others the right to use your idea in return for money.

If you're selling your rights and patent, you'll probably hire a lawyer to help you negotiate the sales terms with potential buyers. You may also use a lawyer to help you apply for the patent.

What to do with Your Children:
What you do with your children will depend on what you're inventing. If you're inventing a product that is to be used by children, you could have your children help you test it out, assuming it would be safe for them to do so.

If you'd like uninterrupted time to work, you could work while your children are napping or at school, or you could have your husband or a babysitter supervise them.

Estimated Time Required:
The time you spend working will depend on what you're inventing. There is no reliable estimate of time required for this income stream.

Estimated Income:
Your income will depend on what you invent and whether or not you keep your rights. There is no reliable estimate of income for this income stream.

Estimated Investment Needed:
What you will need will depend on what you're inventing. Aside from creating the invention itself, you may need to hire a lawyer and pay for a patent. If you're keeping your rights, you will be responsible for the costs of marketing your invention.

Advertising:
Your method of advertising will depend on what you invent and whether or not you keep your rights.

If you plan on selling your rights, you'll need to locate and contact companies that may be interested in purchasing your rights and patent.

If you're marketing the invention yourself, your methods of advertising will depend on what you invent. In general, you could advertise on television, on the radio, in magazines, on billboards, and on newspaper inserts. Word of mouth would be great advertising, too. You could also contact businesses to inquire about them stocking your invention in their stores.

Additional Information and Resources:
The following resources may contain information that you may find helpful for this income stream.
- www.ehow.com/how_2073584_become-inventor.html
- www.ehow.com/how_5178061_become-successful-inventor.html
- www.fabjob.com/inventor.asp
- Inventing on a Shoestring Budget by Barbara Russell Pitts
- Inventing for Dummies by Pamela Riddle Bird and Forrest M. Bird
- Profit from Your Idea: How to Make Smart Licensing Deals by Richard Stim
- The Mom Inventors Handbook: How to Turn Your Great Idea into the Next Big Thing by Tamara Monosoff

Land Surveying

What You'll Do:

As a land surveyor, you'll determine a property's boundaries by measuring distances, angles, and possibly elevations. You'll probably mark the corners of the properties with stakes. You may also provide descriptions and maps of the areas you survey.

You services could be used by builders, residents who want to put a fence around their yard, people who want to subdivide their land, neighbors who dispute their property's boundaries, and many others.

What to do with Your Children:

Your children should not accompany you to your clients' properties. You could have your spouse, another relative, or a babysitter watch your children while you work. If your children are older, you could work while they are in school. Your results need to be accurate, so you can't risk having your children distract you while you're measuring.

Estimated Time Required:

The time required would depend on the demand for your services. There is no reliable estimate for the time required. Some jobs will take longer than others, and your work hours will vary.

Estimated Income:

There is no reliable estimate for your income. It will depend on the demand for your services and the going rate in your area. Around the time of this writing, I believe surveyors earned around $30 per hour.

Estimated Investment Needed:

You will need to be trained. Certification and licensing requirements and fees vary by state. You'll also need various equipment used to survey land and mark boundaries, such as a theodolite on a tripod or a theodolite with an electronic distance measurement device, stakes, and other such things.

Advertising:
You could place an ad in the telephone book. You could also leave business cards at various businesses, especially where manufactured homes are sold.

Additional Information and Resources:
Check the laws, rules, and regulations in your state for surveying requirements.
Some resources that you may find helpful for this business are listed below.
- www.en.wikipedia.org/wiki/Land_surveyor
- www.surveyingcareer.com/careers/salary.html
- www.landsurveyors.com/resources/land-surveyor-license
- www.education-portal.com/land_surveyor_certification.html
- A Guide to Understanding Land Surveys by Stephen V. Estopinal
- Tables and Formulas for the Use of U.S. Surveyors and Engineers On Public Land Surveys: A Supplement to the Manual of Surveying Instructions by United States. General Land Office
- Marketing Professional Services for Land Surveyors by Milton E. Denny

Laundromat Owner

What You'll Do:
 As a Laundromat owner, you'll provide a location that is furnished with coin-operated washing machines and dryers. You won't need to be present during business hours unless you'd like to be. Some people leave their Laundromats unattended during business hours, though that could be asking for trouble or inviting vandalism. Others hire attendants. You'll need to empty the money from the machines, have any necessary repairs made, and keep the facility clean and safe.
 If you'd like, you could sell laundry detergent and dryer sheets there in case any customers forget to bring their own.
 There are numerous potential customers for this business. Anyone without a washing machine is a potential customer. This includes college students, restaurants, and even people whose washing machine is broken at the moment.

What to do with Your Children:
 If you're planning on being at your Laundromat during business hours, you could take your children with you or leave them with your husband or a babysitter. If you're leaving the business unattended, you could bring your children with you or leave them with your husband or a babysitter when you unlock in the morning and close up for the night. If you're paying an attendant to be there for you, you'll only need to bring your children along or find someone to watch them when you go to collect the money from the machines.

Estimated Time Required:
 The amount of time this business will require of you will depend on whether or not you'll be present at the business during business hours. If you'll be hiring an attendant, the time you'll spend working will be extremely minimal.

Estimated Income:

Your income will depend on the number of customers you have and the number of loads of laundry that they wash and dry.

Just as an example though, if you had 5 customers per day, 7 days per week, who each brought 2 loads of laundry and paid $3 for a wash cycle and $3 for a drying cycle, that would earn you around $1800 per month, before deducting your expenses. If you paid an attendant $8 per hour, 40 hours per week, you'd be paying out $1280 per month in wages, though. That is just an example. Your income will vary. If your business is in a good location, you could earn much more than that.

Estimated Investment Needed:

You would need a location for your business, the coin-operated washers and dryers, and any necessary business licenses and permits. You would probably need to take out a business loan to start this business.

You could buy an existing Laundromat instead, if one is available for sale, but you'd still need the licenses and/or permits.

Advertising:

You could hang flyers on college campuses and at grocery stores. You could also place an ad in the telephone book and newspaper.

If your business is in a good location, people will see it when they drive bye it, and they'll surely tell others about the new business they saw.

Additional Information and Resources:

The following resources may contain information that you may find helpful for this business.
- Happiness is Owning a Laundromat: An Introduction to the Coin Laundry Industry by Sally Collins
- Start Your Own Coin-Operated Laundry by Mandy Erickson
- Coin Laundries--Road to Financial Independence: A Complete Guide to Starting and Operating Profitable Self-Service Laundries by Emerson G. Higdon

- How to Start & Manage a Coin-Operated Laundries Business: A Practical Way to Start Your Own Business by Jerre G. Lewis and Leslie D. Renn
- www.ehow.com/how_15362_open-laundromat.html
- www.speedqueen.com/laundromat.htm
- www.laundromatadvisor.com

Laundry Services

What You'll Do:

    Laundry services include machine washing, hand-washing, drying, folding, and possibly ironing. You may pick up the dirty laundry from your customers and deliver the clean laundry to them, which of course you would charge more for, or you may have them drop it off and pick it up from you.

    There are numerous potential customers for this business. You could do laundry for college students, restaurants, motels, single soldiers, or anyone else that doesn't have a washing machine. Even if people have a washing machine, they may not have the time or energy to do their own laundry.

What to do with Your Children:

    Since you already do your own laundry while your children are home, you could certainly do other people's laundry then, too. If you're offering ironing as a service, you'll need to make sure your children are kept away from the hot iron so they don't get burnt. You could do your ironing while your children are napping, at school, at sports practice, or while they're being supervised by your husband or a babysitter.

    If you're picking up and delivering the laundry, your children could ride along with you if there's enough room in your vehicle, if you'd like. If you want to appear more professional though, you could pick up and deliver the laundry while your children are at school, at sports practice, on a playdate, or are being supervised by your husband or a babysitter.

    If your children are old enough, they could help you fold the laundry.

Estimated Time Required:

    The amount of time this business will require of you will depend on the demand for your services, the time it takes your washer and dryer to complete a load of laundry, the speed at which you fold the laundry, and whether or not you'll be delivering or having the laundry picked up. You can estimate the amount of time you'll spend working by using the amount of time you spend on a load of your own laundry as a guide.

To be in control of your schedule, just accept jobs based on the amount of time you'd like to work.

Estimated Income:

Your income will depend on the demand for your services. The rates for laundry services vary, so check around for the going rate in your area. Your pricing options may vary though, depending on whether you charge per load or per item washed.

Just as an example though, if you did 3 loads of laundry per day with each load containing 10 items, 3 days per week, at a rate of $1.50 per item, you'd earn $540 per month. If you did 3 loads of laundry per day, 3 days per week, at a rate of $20 per load, you'd earn $720 per month. Those are just examples though. Your income will vary.

Estimated Investment Needed:

You would need a washer and a dryer, laundry detergent, possibly dryer sheets, possibly an iron, and possibly a drying rack or clothesline. You may also want to invest in reusable cloth bags in which customers can put their dirty laundry for you to pick up. If business is really good, you may even want to invest in an additional washer and dryer to expedite your workload.

Advertising:

You could leave business cards or hang flyers on college campuses, near military bases, at grocery stores, and at restaurants. You could also place an ad in the telephone book and newspaper.

Additional Information and Resources:

The following resources may contain information that you may find helpful for this business.
- www.DormMom.com
- Laundry: The Home Comforts Book of Caring for Clothes and Linens by Cheryl Mendelson

- Betty's Book of Laundry Secrets by Betty Faust and Maria Rodale

Life Coaching

What You'll Do:
      As a life coach, your job will be to help others determine and achieve their goals by instructing them, directing them, and offering motivational support. It is coaching. It is not professional business consulting or therapy. You may help them better manage their time, keep searching for a better career, write a book, or some other goal they may have. They'll talk, and you'll listen. Then, you'll offer your opinion, words of encouragement, or some other type of feedback appropriate for the situation.
      You'll provide one-on-one sessions with your clients either over the telephone or in person. You could charge per session or offer a certain number of sessions per week or month and charge a weekly or monthly fee.

What to do with Your Children:
      Since your clients both desire and deserve your undivided attention and discretion, your children should not accompany you to one-on-one sessions. They also should not be heard in the background during telephone sessions. You may need to accommodate various schedules for your clients, but you could try to do most of your coaching while your children are in school, at a playdate, at sports practice, or napping. You could also have your husband, a babysitter, or another relative supervise your children for you while you work. If your children are adolescents, they should be able to read a book, watch television, or do some other solo activity while you are in another room conducting a telephone session.

Estimated Time Required:
      Coaching sessions will probably last 30 minutes, 45 minutes, or one hour, depending on how long you decide to conduct them. You could even offer 10 or 15-minute mini telephone sessions for clients who just need a quick motivational boost every day or so.

The time you spend coaching will depend on the number of clients you have and the amount of coaching they desire. If you have only 3 clients who desire two 30-minute sessions per week, that would only be three hours per week. That's just an example though.

Decide how much time you want to spend working, and offer sessions of appropriate lengths based on that.

Estimated Income:

Having a life coach generally isn't cheap. At the time of this writing, you could probably earn around $125 per hour, depending on the going rate for coaching in your area. Some coaches charge up to $300 per hour. You could probably charge each client $200-$400 per month for a weekly 30-minute session, though some coaches charge $300-$600. The amount that you charge will probably depend on the going rate in your area, but if you have just 3 clients and charge them each only $200 per month for a weekly 30-minute session, you'll work 6 hours per month and earn a monthly income of $600. That would be $100 per hour. Of course that's just an example though.

Estimated Investment Needed:

There's probably no mandatory investment, but you may want to check into insurance in case you were to be sued by an unhappy client who blames you for his unhappy life.

You could also invest in life coach training. That could range from a few hundred dollars to many thousands of dollars.

Other than that, you'll need a telephone for phone sessions. If you're conducting face-to-face sessions, you'll probably need an office, or you could meet your clients at a restaurant, park, or some other comfortable location.

Advertising:

I highly recommend placing and ad in your telephone book. Since coaching can be done over the telephone, you could also create a website and register your business on online search engines to reach potential clients hundreds and even thousands of miles away.

Additional Information and Resources:

At the time of this writing, the following websites were offering life coach training. There are other places that offer training,

though. Shop around for one that fits your budget, your schedule, and your preferred style of learning.
- www.coachtrainingonline.com/amazon.php for $697
- www.ipeccoaching.com for $8,795

Locksmithing

What You'll Do:
    As a locksmith, you'll make and/or repair locks, and you may have to pick locks to open them. Your services may be needed when people lock themselves out of their house or their vehicle. You may be called upon to change the locks on a business after it's been broken into. You may even have to remove door hinges when someone, probably a child, accidentally locks themselves in a room. You may also make spare keys for existing locks.

What to do with Your Children:
    You should not bring your children with you for this job. You could try to do most of your work while your children are at school, at a playdate, or at sports practice. Since your services may be needed in emergency circumstances or at odd hours, you could have your husband, a babysitter, or another relative supervise your children for you at those times.

Estimated Time Required:
    The time you spend working will depend on the demand for your services, the types of locks involved, and the size and complexity of the job. This job probably won't be full-time.
    Although you could set your hours for pre-scheduled jobs, when someone accidentally locks himself out of his house at night, you may be called to pick the lock for him. If you don't want to be called out for emergency services in the middle of the night, you could turn your ringer off so the telephone doesn't wake your family and leave the number for an alternate locksmith as the greeting on your answering machine. If you do that, though, you will run the risk of losing business.

Estimated Income:
Your income will depend on the demand for your services. Locksmithing fees vary by location, so check around for the going rate in your area, and offer competitive prices.

Estimated Investment Needed:
You'll need to be trained and licensed to be a locksmith. The licensing fee varies by state. The cost of training will vary depending upon the source you use for your training. There are many schools that offer training. Some even offer training via distance learning and include all of the tools needed. Check around for a school that offers a price and curriculum that suit you.

Unless the school at which you receive your training provides the necessary tools, you'll need to buy them. You'll probably need things like a screwdriver, a key making machine, and other locksmithing supplies that will be specified in your training course.

Advertising:
I highly recommend placing and ad in your telephone book. You could also place an ad in the newspaper, pay for radio or television advertisements, and leave business cards at various locations.

Additional Information and Resources:
The following resources may contain information that you may find helpful.
- www.pennfoster.edu/locksmith
- www.en.wikipedia.org/wiki/Locksmithing
- www.nyc.gov/html/dca/html/licenses/062.shtml
- Locksmithing by Bill Phillips
- Mobile Locksmith Company by Tim Roncevich and Steven Primm
- The Complete Book of Locks and Locksmithing by Bill Phillips
- How To Open Locks With Improvised Tools: Practical, Non-Destructive Ways Of Getting Back Into Just About Everything

When You Lose Your Keys (formerly published as Lock Bypass Methods) by Hans Conkel
- The Encyclopaedia for Locksmiths by Mick Friend

Massage Therapy

What You'll Do:

As a massage therapist, you'll provide massage sessions for your clients in your home, at their home, or in a spa or massage parlor. There are many different types of massages you could offer, such as hot stone massages, therapeutic massages, deep tissue massages, and more. You'll learn about the various techniques in your training.

Your clients will probably lie on a massage table, but they may sit in a massage chair. They may be fully clothed, partially clothed, or unclothed and covered by a sheet or towel.

You may use various oils to reduce friction when giving massages. The oils may be scented for aromatherapy.

You could be an independent massage therapist and charge an hourly rate, or you could apply for a job as a massage therapist elsewhere that has flexible hours to meet your needs. Either way, you'll probably earn tips, too.

What to do with Your Children:

Since your clients both desire and deserve your undivided attention and discretion, your children should not accompany you to massage sessions. You could try to book most of your appointments for when your children will be at school, at a playdate, or at sports practice. You could also have your husband, a babysitter, or another relative supervise your children for you while you work.

Estimated Time Required:

Massage sessions will probably last 30 minutes, 45 minutes, or one hour, depending on how long you decide to conduct them. You could even offer 10 or 15-minute mini massage sessions for clients who just need a quick hand or foot massage.

The time you spend working will depend on the demand for your services. If you have only 3 clients who each get a one-hour weekly massage, that would only be three hours per week. That's just an example though. Your hours will vary.

Decide how much time you want to spend working, and schedule the massages based on that. You may need to accept, decline, and postpone appointments to fit your desired schedule.

Estimated Income:
At the time of this writing, you could probably earn anywhere from $50 to $125 per hour, depending on the going rate for massages in your area. Your income will depend not only on your rates, but also on the demand for your services. Just as an example, if you have just 3 clients who each get a one-hour weekly massage, at a rate of $90 per hour, that would be $1080 per month before deducting expenses. Of course that's just an example though. Your income will vary.

Estimated Investment Needed:
You'll need to be trained and licensed. The fees and requirements for that vary by state though. You'll need insurance, too.

You'll also need any necessary furniture and supplies, such as a massage table, oils, stones, towels, etc.

Advertising:
I highly recommend placing and ad in your telephone book. You could also place an ad in the newspaper. You could hang flyers and leave brochures and business cards at various locations, too.

Additional Information and Resources:
The following resources may contain helpful information for this job.
- www.costhelper.com/cost/health/massage.html
- www.en.wikipedia.org/wiki/Massage_therapy
- www.bls.gov/oco/ocos295.htm
- www.ncbtmb.org/
- www.massagetherapy101.com/massage-school/massage-therapy-certification.aspx

- www.alexandarschoolofnatu.homestead.com/Requirementbystate.html
- The Enviable Lifestyle: Creating a Successful Massage Therapy Business by Shelley Johnson
- Massage Therapy Career Guide for Hands-On Success by Steve Capellini

Mobile Search Guide

What You'll Do:
    As a mobile search guide, you'll answer questions that people ask on their mobile phones. You could offer advice or tips, look up a telephone number, tell a joke, or provide any other information for which someone may be looking.
    At ChaCha.com, you'll log on and answer any questions you want. If you don't know the answer, you don't have to answer the question. If it's something you could look up, you could look it up, though. You could specialize in a certain area or field, or you could just answer general questions.
    To be a guide at ChaCha.com, you'll just log on whenever you want, for as long as you want, with no minimum time requirements.

What to do with Your Children:
    You could work from home anytime you have free time from which you won't be distracted. You could work while your children are napping, in bed at night, at school, at sports practice, at a playdate, or even watching television, reading, or playing a game.

Estimated Time Required:
    The time required will depend on the number of questions you answer. Currently, there's no mandatory minimum amount of time required. Just answer as many questions as you want so that you work as much or as little as you want.

Estimated Income:
    At the time of this writing, you could probably earn between $3 and $9 per hour on average. Just decide how much money you want to earn, and answer the amount of questions that it would take for you to earn that much.

Estimated Investment Needed:

You'll need a computer with internet access.

Advertising:
To be a guide at ChaCha.com, you won't need to advertise. You'll just sign up at ChaCha.com to be a guide.

Additional Information and Resources:
Some websites that you may find helpful for this job are listed below.
- www.ChaCha.com
- www.Wikipedia.com
- www.Dictionary.com
- www.Thesaurus.com

Motivational Speaking

What You'll Do:

As a motivational speaker, your job will be to make speeches that motivate others to reach their potential, to better themselves, or to inspire them to make their dreams a reality.

If you've been through a financial hardship, were faced with the decision of whether or not to do drugs, were rejected by a potential mate, or overcome virtually any obstacle in life, you've probably got material to speak about. You'll speak about experiences from your own life, so take an inventory of what you've gone through. Did you achieve your dream, kick a bad habit, start a good habit, overcome a financial hardship, land the perfect job, graduate from college, not give into peer pressure, start your own business, double your investment in the stock market, write a book, or find a suitable mate?

You could speak to students about staying sober or going to college. You could speak to singles about how to stay motivated while looking for the perfect mate. You could speak about real estate investing to people who want to double their income. You could speak to people facing bankruptcy about how you climbed your way out of debt. You could use virtually any life experience you have for your speeches, but you should stick to just one subject. Specialize in something that you're comfortable speaking about, that is a common issue for others, and that will keep your audience motivated.

You could speak at schools, churches, corporations, or you could even book a conference room at a hotel and host your own seminar. There are many locations at which to speak. Choose the ones that fit with your topic.

What to do with Your Children:

Your children probably shouldn't accompany you unless you're speaking to students their age, but even then, it may seem unprofessional to bring them along. You could probably do some of your coaching while your children are at school. For evening and weekend speaking engagements, you could have your husband, a babysitter, or another relative supervise your children for you while you work

Estimated Time Required:

Your speeches will probably last about 45 minutes each. The time you'll spend speaking will depend on the number of speeches you make. If every month you speak at 1 high school and host your own seminar, that would only be about an hour and a half per month, not including travel time. Of course that is just an example though.

Estimated Income:

Your income will depend on the number of engagements at which you speak. If every month you speak at 1 high school for $300 and host your own seminar that attracts an audience of 20 people paying $20 each, you'll earn $700 per month. Of course that is just an example though. You could also boost your income by selling recordings of your speeches or other promotional items at your seminars. The amount that you charge will probably depend on the going rate in your area.

Estimated Investment Needed:

There's probably no mandatory investment, but you will need transportation to and from your speaking engagements. If you're selling promotional items, you'll need to invest in them.

Advertising:

I highly recommend placing and ad in your telephone book. If you don't mind traveling, you could also create a website and register your business on online search engines to reach potential customers at a distance.

Depending on what you're speaking about, you could send flyers to schools, churches, investment companies, or other businesses. You could leave business cards at any appropriate location as well.

If you're hosting your own seminar, you could advertise in the newspaper, on a billboard, and with flyers.

Additional Information and Resources:

The following websites may be helpful for your motivational speaking venture.
- www.becomeamotivationalspeaker.com
- www.motivationalplus.com

Movie Reviewing

What You'll Do:
    As a movie reviewer, you'll critique movies. You'll write your reviews for publication in periodicals or online. It's that simple. You'll watch a movie, write your review, and submit it for publication. You could specialize in reviewing comedies, children's movies, dramas, or some other genre, or you could just review various movies as they debut.
    You could apply for an existing job as a movie reviewer, or you could contact a media outlet to inquire about the possibility of them printing your articles on a regular basis. There are many websites, magazines, and newspapers that print articles of that nature. You could write a weekly column, a monthly blog, or some other scheduled article frequency.

What to do with Your Children:
    If your children can't sit quietly through a movie, or if the movie is too mature for them, you could try to do most of your work while your children are at school, at a playdate, at sports practice, in bed at night, or napping. You could also have your husband, a babysitter, or another relative supervise your children for you while you're watching the movies and/or while you're writing.
    If your children are adolescents, they should be able to read a book, watch television, or do some other solo activity while you are typing, editing, and submitting the review.

Estimated Time Required:
    The time you spend viewing movies will probably range between one and two hours per movie. The amount of movies you view will depend on how often you'll be writing your articles. A weekly column could take a few hours of your time every week. A daily blog could take up 20 hours per week. Those are just examples though. Your hours will vary.

Estimated Income:
Your income will depend on the frequency of your articles and the pay rate of the media outlets that publish them. There is no reliable income estimate without knowing that information.

Estimated Investment Needed:
Other than the cost of the movie tickets and/or rental fees, there's probably no mandatory investment, but you could buy a couple books on the subject if you'd like. If you're an employee of a media outlet, they may reimburse you for your expenses.

Advertising:
You won't be advertising for this job. Instead, you'll search for jobs online and contact various media outlets to inquire about their potential publication of your articles.

Additional Information and Resources:
The following resources may be helpful to you for this job.
- www.fabjob.com/MovieReviewer.asp
- www.en.wikipedia.org/wiki/Movie_reviewer
- Five Stars! How to Become a Film Critic, the World's Greatest Job by Christopher Null

Multi-level Marketing

What You'll Do:
    Multi-level marketing is a marketing structure that compensates the promoter of the products not only for their sales, but also for the sales of the promoters that they recruit. With MLM, when you recruit another person to promote the company's products, that person becomes part of your downline. You'll earn commission on your own sales and the sales of your downline down to a certain level. The structure is a hierarchy structure with multiple levels in the form of a pyramid.
    For example, you may earn 50% commission on your own sales, 40% on the sales of the people that you recruit, and 30% on the sales of the people that they recruit. The commissions and number of levels will vary with different MLM's.
    Not all MLM's are legitimate though, so make sure you thoroughly research a company before deciding to promote their products.

What to do with Your Children:
    You'll appear more professional if your children don't accompany you if you'll be meeting with potential clients. You could meet with clients when your children are at school, being cared for by your spouse, or being watched by a babysitter. You could also make any necessary telephone calls at those times.
    If you're working online, your children could be at home with you. They could be napping, reading, watching television, or even playing a game.

Estimated Time Required:
    The time you spend working will depend on the products you're promoting, the method you use to promote them, and the amount of time you want to put forth to promote them. There is no reliable estimate of the time required for this business without knowing that information.

Estimated Income:
Your income will depend on the number of sales you make, the commission percentage you earn, the number of people in your downline, the number of sales that they make, the number of people that the people in your downline recruit for you, and the number of sales that those people make. There is no reliable estimate of income for this business without knowing those factors. You could probably earn anywhere from a few cents to thousands of dollars.

Estimated Investment Needed:
You may or may not need to put forth an investment for this business. Some companies require you to purchase a start-up kit. Others provide one for you. Some even require you to purchase a minimum volume of their products every month. It will depend on the company you're promoting.

Advertising:
The methods of advertising you use will depend on what you're promoting. You may distribute catalogs, use business cards and brochures, hang flyers, operate a website, or use some other venue of advertising. No matter what you're promoting though, word of mouth would probably be good advertising.

Additional Information and Resources:
I've personally only ever tried one MLM. I was paid monthly and don't have any complaints about it. It was www.Scriptures.com. My husband actually generates extra money via multi-level marketing. His website is www.TravisKMillward.com.
Helpful websites for determining a company's legitimacy are:
- www.MLMwatchdog.com
- www.mlmwatch.org

Music Lessons

What You'll Do:

As a music instructor, you'll teach your students, probably mostly children of various ages, how to play an instrument during one-on-one or small group sessions. Each session will probably last 30 minutes to one hour. You could teach children how to play the piano, the keyboard, the guitar, the clarinet, the violin, or even offer vocal lessons. You could teach any musical talent that you yourself possess.

You'll teach children during your chosen hours after school, on weekends, during the summer, over holiday breaks, or any combination of those times. Since music lessons are usually long-term, most children will be your students for many years.

You can either have the children come to your home or business location for the lessons, or you could go to their homes.

What to do with Your Children:

I suggest one-on-one time with the children you're teaching. If your children are present, they may be a distraction for both you and your students. If you're teaching the lessons at your house, you may want to do so while your children are at a friend or relative's house, while your children are at a playdate, or while your husband takes them for a walk or to the park. You could also teach the lessons while your children are at sports practice, drama club meetings, or some other activity.

If you're going to your students' homes to instruct them, you'll need to leave them with a responsible caregiver.

If you're giving group lessons, your children could be present if they're actively participating as students in the class.

Estimated Time Required:

Music lessons generally last 30 minutes to one hour per day, one to three days per week. The time you'd spend teaching would depend on the number of children you choose to teach and whether you offer private or small group lessons. Just as an example, if you teach private lessons to just two children three days out of the week, assuming that each lesson lasts 45 minutes, that would only be four and a half hours per week. Just decide how much time you want to spend teaching, and accept or decline students based on that.

Estimated Income:

Rates vary by location. At the time of this writing, I've seen lessons ranging from $25 to $75 per session per child.

Just as an example though, if you teach 3 private sessions per week at a rate of $25 per session, you'd earn $300 per month. Of course your income may vary.

Estimated Investment Needed:

There's probably no mandatory investment, but you may want to obtain clearances. Your students will probably provide their own instruments, unless you're teaching piano lessons in your own home.

Advertising:

Tell your friends, neighbors, and fellow parents. If you're well-acquainted with the teachers and faculty at your child's school, you could ask them to recommend you to other parents. Word of mouth is great advertising for music instruction. You could also place an ad in your local newspaper and hang a flyer on the school's bulletin board, and perhaps at a music store.

Additional Information and Resources:

You may want to consider obtaining clearances. That's always a good idea for businesses in which you'll be working with children.

Also, don't advertise as a teacher unless you have a teaching degree. Music instructors don't necessarily need a degree.

Mystery Shopping

What You'll Do:
    As a mystery shopper, you will visit various retailers and report your experience to the company that hired you to visit the businesses. You may visit restaurants, gas stations, clothing stores, financial institutions, and other businesses. You will be given specific instructions about what to observe and report.
    Some things you may be asked to observe are customer service, cleanliness of the establishment, how long it takes to receive your order or check out, the accuracy of your order, and other such things.
    You'll be able to choose what assignments you accept and which ones to decline. There will be a deadline for completing the assignments that you accept.
    Generally, you'll be reimbursed for your purchases up to a certain amount. Sometimes you may be told what to buy and then reimbursed for your purchase and given additional pay for the assignment.
    For some assignments, you'll only get reimbursed, but if you're buying things that you'd normally buy, it'll save you money. Other assignments will reimburse you and pay you an additional amount, thus giving you free products and extra income.

What to do with Your Children:
    Some, if not all assignments, will instruct you to go alone. Since your observations require your full attention, it's best to complete your assignments while your children are at school or being cared for by someone else. Since the assignments don't take long, you could complete one at a restaurant while your husband watches the kids and then bring home your purchase for dinner!

Estimated Time Required:
    You could easily complete most assignments within 20 minutes. If your assignment is for a fast food drive-through, it could

take as little as 5 minutes. If you have to eat at a sit-down restaurant, it could take around an hour.

The total time you spend on your assignments per month will depend on the number of jobs that are available in your area and the number of those jobs that you choose to accept. You can choose your hours by only accepting assignments when you want to work.

Estimated Income:

Different assignments will offer different pay, but it's not unreasonable to expect to get $5-10 worth of free products and $20 pay for an assignment. Sometimes you'll only get pay. Sometimes you'll only get products.

If you complete one paying assignment and one merchandise-only assignment per week, you could easily earn $80, a free pizza, a free fast food value meal, a free sweater, and 5 gallons of free gasoline for your vehicle in a month. That would give you $80 cash and probably up to $80 in free merchandise. That's just an example though. Your income may vary.

Mystery shopping probably won't make you rich, but it could earn you a little extra money, free take-out, and other free items that would save you money.

Estimated Investment Needed:

There's no investment needed for any of the reputable companies I've heard of or registered with. You just create an online account at the mystery shopping website or websites of your choice, wait to be approved, and then choose your assignments. You'll need a computer with internet access. If you don't have that, perhaps you could use the internet for free on a computer at your local library.

Always be leery of a company that tries to charge you to work for them. If they require a registration fee, they may not be legitimate.

Advertising:

Do not advertise for this job. In order for you to accurately report your experience, you're to remain anonymous so that the employees of the businesses you mystery shop at go about business as usual.

Additional Information and Resources:

Some websites that may be of help to you for this income stream are listed below.
- www.ServiceIntelligence.com
- www.AthPower.com
- www.ExperienceExchange.com
- www.workathomenoscams.com/work-from-home-companies

Notary Services

What You'll Do:
    As a notary public, you'll witness people's signatures on various documents, sign the documents as a witness, and apply your official seal. You may witness signatures on wills, powers-of-attorney, deeds, bills of exchange, and other documents.
    People will bring their documents and sign them in your presence. You'll earn a set fee per document, which will be set by the state in which you reside.
    You could offer your services out of your home, or you could inquire with local businesses about being available a few set hours per week at their business to notarize documents there.

What to do with Your Children:
    If you're working from a home office, you could just have a device on the door to alert you when a client enters and only leave the door unlocked during set business hours. If you're doing that, and your husband isn't home to supervise your children while you work, your children may accompany you to your office. After all, they live there too.
    If you're offering your services from home, and you don't have an office, you'll have no choice but to have your children there.
    If you're working at a location other than your home, you'd have to leave your children with your husband, a babysitter, or another qualified caregiver.

Estimated Time Required:
    The amount of time this business will require of you will depend on the demand for your services, but it most likely will not be full-time.
    If the business is in your home, you could have your business open for many hours per day but only have to go into your office when clients come. If you're working outside of your home, decide

how much you want to work, and offer your availability based on that.

Estimated Income:
Your income will depend on the number of documents you notarize and the amount of money you earn per document. There is no reliable estimate for this business without knowing the demand for it. Just as an example, if you notarize 3 documents per week, at $10 each, you'd earn $120 per month. That's just an example though. Your income will vary.

Estimated Investment Needed:
You would need to pay a filing fee. Other requirements, such as bond requirements and examinations, vary by state.

Advertising:
You could place an ad in the telephone book. You could put a business sign in your front yard. You could also contact various businesses, such as banks and car dealerships, to inquire about offering your services there.

Additional Information and Resources:
Don't forget to check your state's regulations regarding becoming a notary public.
You may find some of the following resources helpful for this income stream.
- www.nationalnotary.org
- www.ehow.com/how_11155_become-notary-public.html
- www.en.wikipedia.org/wiki/Notary_public
- How to Start, Operate and Market a Freelance Notary Signing Agent Business by Victoria Ring
- Marketing Advice for Notary Signing Agents by Gerrie Pierre-Fleurimond and Cathy Powell
- Marketing Your Non-Loan Notary Services: Effective and practical techniques to get notary work outside the loan industry by Laura Vestanen
- Mobile Notary Public Company by Tim Roncevich and Steven Primm

- A Treatise on the Law Relating to the Office and Duties of Notaries Public Throughout the United Sta*tes* by John Proffatt

Note Brokering

What You'll Do:
    First, you decide what company you want to work with. In my opinion, Charter Financial is a good company to work with. They provide you with all of the necessary information and training materials, and email and telephone support.
    Then, you will locate notes (mortgage notes, deeds of trust, structured settlements, annuities, etc.), convince the note holder to sell his remaining payments for a lump sum of cash now, and negotiate the buyout amount between the note holder and the note buyer.
    If the note buyer offers, for example, $75,000 to purchase the remaining payments that the note holder would receive, you could offer the note holder $73,000 and net yourself a $2,000 commission. You would be the middle man, and that's how you would earn your commission.
    Notes can be located through public documents recorded in courthouses around the country, and many courthouses allow you to search their documents on their website from the comfort of your home. You may also have people call you offering to sell their notes because they saw your advertisement or business card somewhere.
    An example of a note being created and sold is as follows. A homeowner sells his house using seller-financing. He would act as the bank, accepting monthly payments, similar to rent-to-own but with slightly different paperwork. After receiving a $20,000 down payment, he's receiving the balance of the note in payments of $500 per month at a 7% interest rate for a term of 10 years. After a year, he decides he wants all of his money now, but the mortgage contract (note) created between him and the buyer is not negotiable. He then calls you to request that you buy his remaining payments. You, of course, don't have the money yourself, but you are working with a company that does. You collect all of the necessary information about the note and present it to Charter Financial. They may offer to pay $47,000 for the note. You tell your client the buyout price would

be $44,500. He wants his money now, so he's willing to take a discount and accepts that amount. You inform Charter Financial that he has agreed to accept $44,500. Charter Financial takes over the rest of the buyout process for you. It is completed in about 6 weeks, and the seller of the note receives his $44,500, and you receive your $2,500 commission. Charter Financial then begins receiving the remaining $500 monthly payments that the seller would have received for the remainder of the 10-year term. This is just an example, though. Individual results may vary.

What to do with Your Children:
You could work while your children are napping, sleeping, or even playing. Just don't converse with clients on the telephone if your children can be heard in the background. That would make you seem unprofessional and be a huge turn-off to potential clients. Just let the answering machine pick up if your house is too noisy, and return the call as soon as possible.

Estimated Time Required:
You decide how long you want to spend searching court documents. To make it easier for you, Charter Financial and other companies sell lists of note holders for about $1 per name with a minimum purchase amount.
Most of your business will come from potential clients calling you to sell their notes after seeing your business card or other source of advertising. The time you spend on the telephone should be minimal and probably last less than 10 minutes per call.

Estimated Income:
You should probably earn a minimum of $2,000 per note that you broker, but larger notes will net you more. Don't expect to broker 5 notes a day, though! One note every 6 weeks or so would be a good goal.

Estimated Investment Needed:
At the time of this writing, with Charter Financial, the investment would be $195 for the start-up materials and training kit, plus around $15 shipping, but you'd be reimbursed the $195 when

you brokered your first note. Different companies have different prices though.

You can set the amount of money you want to spend on advertising. You'll also be responsible for the cost of long distance phone calls to clients that are out of your local calling area.

Advertising:

Word of mouth would be great for this business. You should also hand out pamphlets and business cards to banks, realtors, attorneys, and financial planners so they can refer their clients to you. Newspaper advertising would almost certainly catch the eye of potential clients, and hanging flyers on general purpose bulletin boards may bring you potential clients, too.

Additional Information and Resources:

www.CharterNotes.com is the website address for Charter Financial.

www.VistaPrint.com is a website where you could customize free and inexpensive promotional items such as business cards, flyers, brochures, key chains, and other items.

www.Freeservers.com is a site at which you can create your own website.

Online Auctions and Fixed-price Listings

What You'll Do:

Online shopping is very popular. Online auctions are especially appealing to people looking to save money or buy an item that may be difficult to find. Most online auction sites that I've come across allow you to sell both new and used items.

To sell items online, you should find an auction site on which you'd be interested in selling. Review the current listings for ideas of what to sell. If you already know what you want to sell, review the listings to see how much those things are listed for and the average sale price. You'll then need to register with the site, if you haven't already, and get something to sell. You'll take photos of what you're selling to be displayed in the listing. To list your item, you'll write a title and a description, upload a photo of it, and state the price and shipping charges. Some sites allow you to choose how many days the listing will run. Some allow you to have a fixed-price listing instead of an auction.

Once the item you have listed sells, and the buyer pays, usually through paypal, you'll package the item and mail it. You can either print postage online, or go to the post office or other delivery service to ship your sales.

You can list multiple items for sale at the same time, which I recommend since sales generate your income.

Most, if not all, online auction sites charge fees, so be sure to figure those costs into your projected earnings.

What to do with Your Children:

Since you'll be working online, you probably won't need to worry too much about what to do with your children. You can sit at a table with a laptop and work while your children sit at the table and color. You could also package your sales at the table, too.

If you have trouble concentrating while your children are around, you could work while they're napping, at school or sports practice, or even when they're asleep at night. Online auction sites are open 24 hours a day, 7 days a week.

If you're having the packages picked up from your home by a shipping service, you won't need to do anything different with your children than you already do. If you're taking the packages to the shipping service to be mailed or delivered, you can either bring your children with you, or go when they're in school or while your spouse or another caregiver is home with them.

Estimated Time Required:

The time required would depend on your inventory. If your inventory is readily available to you, it will obviously take less time than if you had to search in different locations to find the items you're selling. If you have to drive to a certain store to buy the things you're going to sell, you'll need to figure driving time into the time you'll spend working, too. If you're making items, such as crafts or jewelry, to sell, you'll need to figure in the production time as well.

It's safe to assume that you won't spend more than 15 minutes to list an item and 5-10 minutes to package it and print out the postage. If you're driving the item to a shipping service or post office, you'll need to figure how long that will take, too.

There are many factors involved in figuring the amount of time required for this business, too many to give a reliable estimate without having more information. To be in control of your schedule, just work as much or as little as you can or want to.

Estimated Income:

Your income will depend on the number of items you sell and the income earned per item after any applicable fees are deducted.

Just as an example, if you sell 3 items per week for $20 each and pay fees of $3 per item, you would end up with $54 per week. You'd also end up with $54 per week if you sold 12 items for $5 each and paid fees of 50 cents per item. Your income may vary though.

You could earn a few dollars, $100, or even $1,000. It all depends on your sales.

Estimated Investment Needed:
You'll definitely need a computer with internet access. If you're printing postage online, you'll need a printer, ink cartridges, and either printer paper and tape, or the proper size of printable adhesive labels. For photos, you'll either need a digital camera with a USB cable, or for smaller items you may be able to use a scanner for the pictures.

You could buy packaging supplies if you wanted or needed to. You'll almost definitely need tape, but instead of buying other supplies, you could package the items in used boxes or paper bags, and you may be able to use crumpled up newspaper instead of bubble wrap.

You'll also need money to buy the things you're going to sell, or to buy the materials needed to make your inventory, but the amount of money needed will depend on what you're going to sell.

Advertising:
Advertising generally isn't necessary. If you're selling random things, you could tell a few friends. If you're selling a specialty item, you could print a few business cards and leave them at places that may be interested in what you're selling.

Additional Information and Resources:
Websites that may be helpful:
- www.ebay.com
- www.etsy.com
- www.paypal.com
- www.auctions.yahoo.com
- www.ubid.com
- www.bidfind.com

Online Customer Service Representative

What You'll Do:

As an online customer service representative, you'll assist customers via online chat or by telephone. You'll log into the website of the company for which you're working and begin assisting customers with their comments, product orders, questions, requests, or other customer service issues. You'll sit at your home computer and use it to look up customer issues on the company's website. You'll be able to access information that they don't have access to themselves.

The employment may be temporary or long-term.

What to do with Your Children:

Since this is an online job, you could work from home anytime you have free time, though employers will want to know ahead of time what hours you'll be working so that they can make sure they won't have too few or too many customer service representatives available at any certain time. You could work while your children are napping, in bed at night, at school, at sports practice, at a playdate, or even being supervised by your husband or another responsible caregiver. You won't need to work the same hours every day, or even every week. Your schedule can generally vary based on your availability.

Estimated Time Required:

The time required will depend on the company for which you choose to work. You may be able to work as little as a couple hours per month if you wanted to. Most companies will probably require a minimum amount of hours in a given time period. They'll probably also state a maximum number of hours as well. This job probably wouldn't be full-time unless you wanted it to be.

Estimated Income:
　　　The pay range for customer service representatives starts at minimum wage and goes up from there. It's not a job that'll make you rich, but it could be a nice boost to your current income. Just as an example, if you worked 2 hours per day, 3 days per week, at a rate of $9 per hour, you'd earn $216 per month. If you worked 1 hour every day in a 30-day month, at $9 per hour, you'd earn $270. If you wanted to work more, 20 hours per week at $9 per hour would put your monthly income up to $720. Those are just examples though. Your schedule and income will vary based on your wishes.

Estimated Investment Needed:
　　　You will need a computer, internet access, and probably a headset telephone. The company for which you work may require you to pay for the background check that they run on you, and they may require you to have a separate telephone line to use only for business purposes. The requirements will vary from company to company, so check around before deciding on a company for which to work.

Advertising:
　　　You won't need to advertise for this job. You'll simply apply with whatever company or companies for which you wish to work.

Additional Information and Resources:
　　　Some websites that you may find helpful for this income stream are listed below.
- www.LiveOps.com
- www.WorkAtHomeAgent.com
- www.VIPDesk.com
- www.Convergys.com
- www.WestAtHome.com
- www.MagicJack.com
- www.workathomenoscams.com/work-from-home-companies

Online Paid Surveys

What You'll Do:
 To earn income from online paid surveys, you'll register with various websites that pay you to take their surveys. They may email you alerts containing links to the surveys, or you may just search the survey website for surveys to take.
 Some surveys may be targeting a certain demographic, so you may or may not be eligible to take them. For the surveys that you do take, you'll just answer honestly, giving your opinion about whatever the survey is about.

What to do with Your Children:
 Since this is an online job, you could work from home anytime you have free time. You could work while your children are napping, in bed at night, at school, at sports practice, at a playdate, or even watching television or playing a game.
 If you're able to focus, you could even sit at the computer and take surveys with your children on your lap.

Estimated Time Required:
 The time required will depend on the number of surveys you take. There's no reliable estimate for the time required since the number of surveys for which you qualify may vary from time to time, but it shouldn't take up very much of your time. Just take surveys for as long and as often as you feel like working.

Estimated Income:
 Your income will depend on the number of surveys you take and the amount of money you earn per survey. Some surveys may pay $1. Some may pay $5. It will vary. If, for example, you take two $3 surveys per day, you'd earn $42 per week, or around $180 per month. That's just an example though. Your income will vary.

Estimated Investment Needed:
You will need a computer and internet access, but if you don't have that, you could go to your local library or some other place that offers free internet access.

Advertising:
You won't advertise for this business. Instead, you'll register with online paid survey websites.

Additional Information and Resources:
Some websites that you may find helpful are listed below.
- www.surveysavvy.com
- www.acop.com
- www.mysurvey.com

Operating a Paid to Click Website

What You'll Do:
　　As a paid to click website owner, you'll sell advertising on your site to various other website owners. Their sites could be of any genre. They could be retail websites, online matchmaking sites, ebook sales, or some other type of business. The people purchasing advertising credits will furnish you with their pre-made ads for you to display on your site.

　　Then, you'll pay people who visit your site to click on the ads, watch the video ads, or to just view the ads. Minimum viewing time is usually 10-15 seconds per ad to make sure the clickers actually read at least a little of it. The goal is to get the clickers to visit the sites being advertised and earn a commission on the sales that you refer. Every time they click, another advertisement will load. They'll continue clicking and viewing advertisements, and hopefully at least one will entice them to make a purchase.

　　To earn more money than you pay out, you'll charge more for the advertising credits that you sell than you'll pay for having them clicked on. For example, if you sell advertising credits for five cents each, you'll only pay about one or two cents for every time someone clicks on them.

　　When operating a paid to click site, you'll earn money on the sale of advertising credits and commissions on the purchases made by those people who click on the ads on your site.

What to do with Your Children:
　　Since this is an online job, you could work from home anytime you have free time. You could work while your children are napping, in bed at night, at school, at sports practice, at a playdate, or even watching television or playing a game.

If you need additional time to work, you could have your husband supervise your children while you work, or you could hire a babysitter.

Estimated Time Required:
The time required will depend on the number of customers you have, the amount of customer support inquiries you receive and respond to, your computer knowledge and skills, and whether or not you hire a professional to help with various aspects of your site, such as graphics, outlay, etc. There's no reliable estimate for the time required without knowing those factors.

Estimated Income:
Income for this type of business varies greatly. It's not possible to estimate the income from this income stream without knowing the price you'll be charging for advertisements, the price you'll be paying for clicks, and your potential commission percentages.

Estimated Investment Needed:
You will need a computer and internet access. You'll also need a website. You could build one yourself, pay someone else to build it for you, or purchase a pre-made site. You'll also need to pay the people who click.

Advertising:
Your advertising will mostly be online. You could advertise through affiliates, purchase ad space on other sites, or buy advertising credits on other paid-to-click sites.

Additional Information and Resources:
Some websites that you may find helpful are listed below.
- www.simplweb.com/membership-websites
- www.getpaidwithaclick.blogspot.com
- www.clickconsult.com

Packing

What You'll Do:
    As a professional packer, you'll simply pack things. I would recommend contacting your local moving companies to inquire about the services they offer. Some pack and haul a person's belongings. Some only haul the belongings. If you find one that only hauls a person's belongings and leaves the packing up to the individual, you can inquire about the possibility of them utilizing your services.
    Some companies may be willing to use you as an independent contractor. They would tell you of a job that needs done, you would do it, and they would pay you after taking their portion of the profits. Other companies may not be interested in contracting with you, but they may be willing to let you leave business cards and hang flyers for your business in their office.
    If you do contract with a moving company, it may be wise for you to have employees or partners to complete jobs that you don't have the time for. That way, your business will never have to turn down a packing job.
    Make sure to pack other's items carefully. You'll be responsible for anything that gets broken during packing. You'll most likely have your business insured, and I highly recommend doing so, but too many insurance claims can raise the price of your insurance policy. Although the movers may be responsible for breaking some items, sometimes it may be difficult to determine if the damage was caused by poor packing or careless movers, so purchase insurance just to be safe.
    Although you'll pack a person's belongings, the movers will load them and deliver them. You won't need to unpack them because the individual will want to decide where he or she wants his or her things to be in his or her new home.

What to do with Your Children:
    You will definitely not want to bring your children with you for this job unless they are teenagers employed by you. Accidents

happen, and it would be all too easy for one of your children to accidentally knock over a lamp or valuable vase.

You may be able to pack all the items in an uncluttered house in one day while your children are at school. During summer break and on weekends, you'll need to hire a babysitter or make other arrangements for your children to be supervised. If you have employees, you could always have them take care of the summer and weekend jobs so that you don't have to hire a babysitter. It'll cost you money either way, though. Either you'll pay a babysitter or one of your packing employees. Just go with whichever one works best for you and your family.

Estimated Time Required:

The time you spend working will depend on the number of clients you have, the amount of possessions they have, the amount of clutter they have, and the speed at which you can pack. Your hours will vary.

It's not unreasonable to believe that you could pack a house-worth of belongings during the part of the day when your children are at school, but if you're working alone, be sure not to book more than one job per day. If you have help, the process will go a lot faster. After your first job, you'll have a good idea of the amount of time most of your future jobs will take.

Estimated Income:

Your income will depend on your rates, the number of jobs for which you're hired, and the amount you pay any employees you may have. Your income will vary.

For example, you may have 2 jobs you do yourself, and 2 jobs that you have help with per month. If you charge your clients each $250 per job, and pay your employees each $75 per job, with one employee helping you, you'd earn $850 per month. With 2 employees helping you, you'd earn $700 per month. However, those figures don't include the cost of insurance for your business or the cost of packing materials.

Estimated Investment Needed:

You would need to purchase insurance for your business. You would probably want to have business cards and flyers made, and possibly take out an ad in a newspaper or your local yellow pages directory.

You'll also need packing supplies. You'll probably need to buy the tape and bubble-wrap, but you may be able to acquire boxes for free from local businesses, especially from restaurants and grocery stores on the days they receive their food deliveries. If not, you'll need to buy boxes, too, but buying them in bulk should save you a significant amount of money.

Advertising:

Hanging flyers and leaving business cards at moving companies and real estate offices would be great advertising. You could also put an ad in your local newspaper and telephone book directory.

Additional Information and Resources:

A few websites to compare prices of packing supplies are listed below. For an insurance quote for your business, try Erie Insurance or any other reputable insurance company. You may get the best rate using a small, local insurance agency.

- www.packing.com
- www.fast-pack.com
- www.packnseal.com

Paid Membership Websites

What You'll Do:
 As a paid membership website owner, you'll own one or more websites on which only people who register and pay a monthly fee will have access. Your website(s) could have virtually any theme or information available. On your site(s), you could offer online coupon codes, recipes, stock tips, parenting advice, marriage resources, e-books, internet marketing resources, or some other information.
 Since you'll be receiving a monthly fee from the members, you'll need to update the site(s) at least monthly. You could offer new information, resources, products, or all three. You'll need to keep your members coming back so they'll stay subscribed to your website(s).

What to do with Your Children:
 Since this is an online job, you could work from home anytime you have free time. You could work while your children are napping, in bed at night, at school, at sports practice, at a playdate, or even watching television or playing a game.
 If you need additional time to work, you could have your husband supervise your children while you work, or you could hire a babysitter.

Estimated Time Required:
 The time required will depend on the type of resources your site(s) will be offering, the amount of customer support inquiries you receive and respond to, your computer knowledge and skills, and whether or not you hire a professional to help with various aspects of your site, such as graphics, outlay, etc. There's no reliable estimate for the time required without knowing those factors.

Estimated Income:

Income for this type of business varies greatly. It's not possible to estimate the income from this income stream without knowing the type of site(s) you'll be operating, your projected audience, your subscription fees, and the cost of any additional products you may be offering.

Estimated Investment Needed:
You will need a computer and internet access. You'll also need a website. You could build one yourself, pay someone else to build it for you, or purchase a pre-made site. You'll also need information or resources for your site. You could create them yourself or hire professional content writers.

A big part of your success in this business will be your marketing strategy. If you're using affiliates, you'll need to pay them a commission for the referrals they send you that result in sales. You may also pay for other online advertising.

Advertising:
Your advertising will be mostly online. You could advertise through affiliates, purchase ad space on other sites, or buy advertising credits on paid-to-click sites.

Depending on the theme of your site, you may also want to hand out business cards or hang flyers at other businesses that have customers that may be interested in what you have to offer. Word of mouth and an ad in a telephone book or newspaper may be helpful, too.

If you want to advertise really big, you could pay to rent ad space on a billboard.

Additional Information and Resources:
Some websites that you may find helpful for this income stream are listed below.
- www.launchformulamarketing.com
- www.membershipsiteadvisor.com
- www.memberstar.com/home.php?varset=s:1-pm:p
- www.wildkatana.com/blog/how-build-a-paid-membership-website-using-drupal
- www.simplweb.com/membership-websites

Painting

What You'll Do:
    As a painter, you'll paint the interior, and possibly exterior, of your clients' homes. You may need to prep the surfaces before you paint. You'll paint walls, trim, ceilings, and possibly cabinets. You could also paint or refinish furniture, such as dressers, tables, and chairs. Painting the exterior of houses will probably be rare for you due to vinyl siding, but you may paint or stain porches and decks. You may also paint or stain wooden swing sets, pool decks, wooden sidewalks, fences, patio furniture, benches, and other lawn accents.
    Most likely, you'll offer paint samples from which your clients can choose their preferred color. You'll purchase the paint and other necessary items, but you will probably receive a deposit from your clients before you purchase those supplies.
    Your clients may or may not be home when you paint. It may be easier if they're not home, but some people may not feel comfortable allowing others in their homes when they're not present.
    If you're painting a home's interior, keep everything in the house private. Don't tell anyone about expensive electronics that may invite a burglar. Don't gossip about medication bottles you see that may embarrass your client. If the house is dirty, don't embarrass your clients by telling others how unsanitary you found the environment to be. Your job is just to paint, not to snoop, judge, or gossip. Your clients' lives should remain private.

What to do with Your Children:
    Your children should not accompany you to your clients' homes. You could have your spouse, another relative, or a babysitter watch your children while you paint. If your children are older, you could work while they are in school.

Estimated Time Required:
   The time required would depend on the size and intricacy of the surface that you're painting and the speed at which you paint. After the first time you paint, you'll have a good idea of how long it'll take the next time.

Estimated Income:
   Your income will depend on the number of clients you have and the amount you charge for your services. The amount you charge will depend on the going rate in your area.

Estimated Investment Needed:
   You'll need paint samples, paint, masking tape, paintbrushes, a tray, a roller, drop cloths, a bucket, and possibly a paint sprayer and paint thinner. You should also purchase insurance. You may or may not need other items depending on the jobs you're doing. For example, if you're sponge painting, you'll need a sponge.

Advertising:
   You could also advertise in the newspaper and place an ad in the telephone book. You could also leave business cards at home improvement stores and real estate offices.

Additional Information and Resources:
   Some resources that you may find helpful for this business are listed below.
- Smart Guide: Painting: Interior and Exterior Painting Step by Step by Editors of *Creative Homeowner*
- Painting Your House Inside and Out: Tips and Techniques for Flawless Interiors and Exteriors by Bonnie Rossier Krims and Judy Ostrow
- Weekend Painter's DVD. How to Paint Like a Pro!
- www.amazon.com
- www.lowes.com

Party Planning

What You'll Do:
    As a party planner, you'll meet with clients to discuss the event that they want you to plan for them. It may be a 50th anniversary party, an engagement party, a bridal shower, a bachelorette party, a high school reunion, a graduation party, a corporate Christmas party, a bar mitzvah, a sweet 16 party, a family reunion, a baby shower, or some other type of celebration. You'll discuss the budget, the theme, the location, the music or entertainment, the menu, and everything else that pertains to their special event.
    You'll probably compile a portfolio of possible locations, florists, caterers, musicians, entertainers, and other services that may be relevant to a party for your clients to browse through for options. You could also create a portfolio of pictures of parties you've planned, along with letters of recommendation to show to your potential clients.
    Once you have all of the information that you need from your clients, you'll arrange the perfect celebration for them. You'll book the caterer, the entertainment, and everything else that needs taken care of. You will be in charge of making sure that the party is exactly as your clients want it to be.
    Don't forget to get a deposit for the services you'll be booking for your clients. You certainly wouldn't want to have to pay out of pocket for them.

What to do with Your Children:
    Since your clients deserve your full attention, and because it's unprofessional to bring your children along to meetings, it's best to meet with clients while your children are at school or being cared for by someone else. If they won't be a distraction to you, you could book the appropriate venues for the parties at home even while your children are present.

Estimated Time Required:
There is no reliable estimate of the amount of time required for this business since every party is different. It will depend on the type of party and how elaborate your clients want it to be. Think back to parties you've planned before, even if it was just a simple birthday party, to get an estimate of the time involved.

Estimated Income:
Income varies greatly for this job. You'll charge either a percentage of the total cost of the party, a flat fee, or an hourly rate. Your income will depend on the number of clients you have, the cost of the parties or the rate you charge for your services, and the amount of time you spend planning. Check around for the going rate for party planners in your area, and offer a competitive rate.

Just as an example though, if you plan 2 parties per month and earn $500 per party, your monthly income would be $1,000. Of course your income will vary.

Estimated Investment Needed:
You'll definitely need a telephone for all of the calls you'll need to make. The cost of creating a portfolio should be minimal. You could work from home, but if you'd like to rent office space you could. Although you'll need to put a deposit on the services you reserve for the parties, you could charge your clients up front for those expenses instead of paying out of pocket for them.

This shouldn't be a very costly business to start.

Advertising:
I highly recommend placing an ad in the telephone book. You could also place an ad in the newspaper. You could leave business cards at flower shops, party supply stores, bakeries, restaurants, or virtually any other business. You could also create a website for your business. If you wanted to advertise really big, you could rent a billboard.

Additional Information and Resources:
Some websites that you may find helpful for this business are listed below.
- www.PartyPop.com

- www.en.wikipedia.org/wiki/Event_planning
- www.BestPartyEver.com
- www.MyPartyPlanner.com
- www.Party411.com

Personal Chef

What You'll Do:

As a personal chef, you'll provide meals for your clients based on their needs and desires. You'll either be given a meal plan by your clients, or you'll submit one to them for approval. Once the meal plan is approved, you'll be given a deposit. You'll shop for the ingredients, bring them back to your clients' homes, and prepare the food for them there. Occasionally, a chef may prepare the food in her own kitchen, but it must have passed an official health inspection before she can do that.

You may provide a week's worth of meals or perhaps just a few meals at a time. Once they're prepared, you'll put them in appropriate containers and either refrigerate them or freeze them for your clients to consume at a later date. It would be a good idea to put labels on the containers that state what's in them and the date that they were prepared. Once the meals are finished, you'll receive the remainder of your pay and possibly even a tip.

You may provide meals for single men, busy families, women who don't like to cook, couples who want a special occasion dinner, or others. The clients for this business are very diverse.

What to do with Your Children:

You could do this job while your children are at school. If your children are too young for school, or if it is summer break, you could hire a babysitter or leave them with your spouse while you prepare the meals. As long as you can focus on your grocery list and keep your children from damaging the products, it probably wouldn't hurt to take them to the grocery store with you if you wanted to while you shop for the ingredients.

Estimated Time Required:

The time required will depend on what you're cooking, how many meals you're cooking, and the number of clients that you have.

If you're slow roasting a pot roast, of course you'll be at your client's house for hours. If you're making grilled salmon on a bed of wilted greens, you won't be there near as long.

There's no reliable estimate for how much time you'll spend working without knowing the preparation and cook times for the foods you're cooking. Look at your recipes to determine how long it will take you, but don't forget to also figure in the time it'll take you to shop for the groceries and clean up the kitchen.

Estimated Income:
The going rate for personal chefs will probably vary depending on the area in which you live and the demand for your services. Check to see what other personal chefs in your area are charging, and then offer a competitive price.

Of course your income will depend on how much you charge and the number of clients you have. As an estimate at the time of this writing, you may be able to earn $25 to $50 per hour plus the cost of food, but you may earn more or less than that depending on the going rate in your area.

Estimated Investment Needed:
You may or may not need to make an initial investment. If you've got experience, great. If not, you may want to take a class or receive some personal training. Check with your local government authority to find out if you'll need any licenses, certifications, or any other requirements.

Advertising:
You could place an ad in the telephone book and your local newspaper, and hang flyers at grocery stores, gyms, and other locations. Word of mouth would be great, too.

Additional Information and Resources:
Check with your local government authority to find out the rules and regulations regarding food preparation and sales in your area. Below are some websites you may find helpful.
- www.personalchef.com
- www.uspca.com
- www.personalchefsummit.com

Personal Scrapbooking

What You'll Do:
As a personal scrapbooker, you'll preserve your clients' memories in an album on pages decorated with photographs, news clippings, small mementos, or other decorations. The photographs and newspaper clippings would be provided by your clients, and sometimes some of the decorations may be provided by them as well. You may or may not provide the album, but most likely, you'll provide the pages and the bulk of the accents.

If you'd like to expand your services to create an even larger income, you could host scrapbooking classes, too!

What to do with Your Children:
Some children may be able to be entertained by watching you scrapbook. Others may try to be a little too helpful. If you're scrapbooking in the presence of your children, make sure they don't damage anything.

If you'd rather work while you're alone and undistracted, you'll have to work while your children are napping, at school, being entertained by your spouse or other family member, on a playdate, at sports practice, or even in bed for the night or before they wake in the morning.

As for having your children around when you're scrapbooking, if you're working at a large table, you could always allow your children to make a craft or work on their own scrapbooks at the other end. As long as your clients are happy with your work, your children being there shouldn't matter to them.

Estimated Time Required:
The time you'll devote to this business will depend on the demand for your services, the pace at which you work, and the intricacy of the details desired on the pages. This probably won't be a full-time job. You could work as little as an hour per week, or you

could work many hours per day. There is no reliable estimate for this until you actually get started with it.

Estimated Income:
Your income will depend on the number of pages you create and the amount you charge per page. Rates vary in different areas, so check the going rate in your area, and set a competitive price based on those rates and your desired income.

Just as an example, if you charge $5 per 12"x12" page, a scrapbook of 20 pages would earn you $100. At $3 per 8"x8" page, with 2 clients who each want 20 pages created, you'd earn $120. Your rates may be higher, but using that as an example, one 12"x12" scrapbook per week could earn you $400 per month before deducting the cost of materials. Those are just examples though. Your income will vary.

Estimated Investment Needed:
You will need to purchase scrapbooking pages, decorations and accents, and possibly scrapbooking albums. Glue and double-sided tape will probably be necessary. You'll also need scissors and possibly other various scrapbooking materials.

Advertising:
You could leave business cards at party supply stores, photography studios, craft stores, jewelry stores, toy stores, flower shops, and bridal shops. You could hang flyers on bulletin boards at malls.

You could advertise in the newspaper and telephone book, too.

Word of mouth would be great advertising, especially if it came from a happy customer.

Additional Information and Resources:
The following websites contain information that you may find helpful for this business.
- www.pagesbyheather.com
- www.scrapbooking.com
- www.scrapbook.com
- www.scrapbooking.about.com

The following books may contain helpful information for your scrapbooking venture.
- The Amazing Page: 650 Scrapbook Page Ideas, Tips and Techniques by Memory Makers
- Scrapbook Page Maps: Sketches For Creative Layouts by Becky Fleck
- 601 Great Scrapbook Ideas by Memory Makers

Personal Shopping

What You'll Do:
    As a personal shopper, you'll shop for anything and everything your clients desire. Their lists may include clothing for themselves, jewelry for a loved one, or even just groceries. If you shop for clothing, you'll probably be given specifics such as size, style, color, and fabric of the item desired, and the amount of money they're willing to spend on it. As a personal shopper though, if your clients don't like what you buy them, you'll have to return those purchases. You'll need to really understand your clients. If you continuously bring them items they don't like, you won't have a job for very long.
    You may end up buying clothing for executives, groceries for busy housewives, promotional items for businesses, or anything else that can be purchased in a store.
    Generally, you'll be reimbursed for your purchases, but sometimes you may be given the money ahead of time. Either way, you'll receive more than the actual purchase costs you because you'll be being paid for your service of shopping for the items.

What to do with Your Children:
    You'll want to meet with clients when your children are at school or being cared for by someone else, and you probably shouldn't bring them along on your shopping trips either. This would be a great job for when your children are at school.

Estimated Time Required:
    The time required will depend on the number of clients you have, the number of items they want you to purchase, and the amount of time it takes you to complete the purchases. Grocery shopping could take a couple hours. Finding the perfect dress could take minutes or hours. There is no reliable estimate of the time required for this job.

Estimated Income:

You'll probably charge your clients either an hourly rate for your services, or a percentage of the purchase. Your rates will depend on the going rate in your area and the demand for your services.

If you charged 15% of the purchase price, a $250 grocery shopping trip would earn you $37.50 no matter how long it took you to buy the groceries. If you charged an hourly fee of $15, that same trip would earn you $30 if it took you 2 hours. That's just an example though. Your income will vary depending on your rates and how much business you have.

Estimated Investment Needed:

There's probably no mandatory investment needed. You'll be providing a service, so you'll just need to find people to pay you for it. There's no inventory or formal training required. You may need to pay for transportation if you're not within walking distance of the shopping locations.

Advertising:

You could place an ad in the telephone book and newspaper. You could leave business cards at gyms, doctors' offices, toy stores, spas, grocery stores, and any other businesses that you think may have customers that may be interested in your services. Word of mouth would be great advertising, too.

Additional Information and Resources:

You can find more information online. A couple websites that you may find helpful are listed below.

- www.fabjob.com/PersonalShopper.asp
- www.moneymakingmommy.com/ideas/becoming-a-personal-shopper.htm

Pet Sitting

What You'll Do:
    Sometimes when people pet sit, they bring the pets they're watching while the owners are gone to their own house. Since you have kids, you may or may not want to do that depending on how comfortable you, your children, and the animals are with the children and animals interacting with each other. Dogs may bite, cats may scratch, and someone in your family could have a pet dander allergy. Always keep safety in mind when making your decision. To pet sit, you just take over the day-to-day responsibilities of caring for the animals.
    Generally, you'll feed and water the animals. You may need to take dogs out for a walk or let them out to go to the bathroom a couple times a day. You'll need to clean up their mess when they go outside. You may need to change a letter box, check the ph of fish tank water, or change the newspaper in the bottom of a bird cage. It's like temporarily having your own pet, and probably leaving it at someone else's house.
    The owners will probably leave you with a key to their house and tell you what needs to be done, how much food and water to give, and at what time(s) or how often.
    If you'd like to do this on a larger scale, you could open a kennel.

What to do with Your Children:
    If you and the pets' owner think it's safe to bring your children around the animals, you could bring them with you.
    If your children nap, you could have their father, grandmother, or a neighbor come over while you sneak out to fulfill your pet sitting responsibilities. If they're old enough to stay alone, you could leave them at home for the half hour or so that it would take you to care for the animals.
    You could also care for the animals while your children are at school.

Estimated Time Required:
You would need to check on the animals everyday that their owners are gone. It may only take you 20 minutes. If you have to walk a dog, it may take an hour. You may come and go multiple times in a day.

On average, you could probably spend only up to one or two hours per day caring for the animals, but the amount of time you spend working will vary.

Estimated Income:
Your income would depend on your duties. For example, you would be paid more if you had to walk a dog multiple times a day.

Just as an example, if you were paid $25 per day, and the owners were gone for 3 days, you'd earn $75. If you did that twice a month, you'd have a monthly income of $150. Business would probably be sporadic though, so your income would vary from month to month.

Estimated Investment Needed:
If you have to drive to the house where the pets are, you'll have to pay for the gas in your car. Other than that, you shouldn't have any investment costs.

Advertising:
Most people will only hire people that they know to pet sit for them. Word of mouth would be the best advertising for you. Tell your friends. After you've pet sat for a few acquaintances, they may recommend your services to people that they know, thus giving you credibility and making you appear trustworthy to strangers.

Additional Information and Resources:
You could call your local humane society or veterinarian with any questions you may have regarding pet care.

Photography

What You'll Do:
    As a photographer, you'll simply take photographs with a camera. In this day and age, you'll use a digital camera, preferably of high quality. You can deliver the photos as prints, though you could also deliver them as files on a computer disc. If you're not printing the photographs yourself, you could use an online photo center to print them.
    You could contract to take photographs at special events such as weddings, graduations, proms, and family reunions. You could sell photographs to magazines. You could also take photos for newspapers and real estate agents or be the photographer for school yearbook photos.

What to do with Your Children:
    If you have a room at home to use as your studio for still shots, you could have your husband care for your children, or you could hire a babysitter to supervise them while you work.
    If you have to leave the house to go to the location, you'll need to go while your children are being supervised by your husband, a babysitter, or another qualified caregiver. Sometimes you may be able to work while your children are at school.

Estimated Time Required:
    The time required will depend on the number of clients you have and the kind of photos they desire. You could work half an hour photographing a house for a real estate agent, 5 hours at a wedding, 8 hours for school yearbook photos, or some other amount of time. There is no reliable estimate for the time required, but it probably won't be full-time unless you want it to be. Just accept, postpone, and decline jobs based on the amount of time you have available to work.

Estimated Income:
Your income will depend on the type of job you're doing. Weddings may be quite lucrative. Real estate photos may be less lucrative. Check around for other photographers' rates in your area, and charge a competitive price.

Estimated Investment Needed:
You'll definitely need a camera for this job. You'll probably also need extra storage for your digital camera, such as a memory card. Depending on the type of photos you'll be taking, you may need lighting and props, too. You may also need various other items such as tripods and batteries.

Advertising:
You could place an ad in the telephone book. You could leave business cards at bridal shops, party supply stores, and other relevant locations. You could also send letters or brochures to schools and real estate offices. Additionally, you could set up a website to display sample photos and offer your contact information.

Additional Information and Resources:
You may want to check into your copyright rights.
Some websites that you may find helpful for this business are listed below.
- www.ppa.com
- www.copyright.gov/help/faq/faq-fairuse.html
- www.pennfoster.edu/photobasics-cert
- www.en.wikipedia.org/wiki/Photographer

Placemat Advertising

What You'll Do:
You've probably seen placemats with numerous business ads on them. Some have ads all the same size. Some have ads of different sizes to fit different businesses' budgets. With placemat advertising, you'll sell advertising space on placemats, possibly have the placemats formatted, have the placemats printed, and give the placemats to restaurants that will use them. It should be relatively easy to find restaurants that will use the placemats because not many of them will decline free placemats. Of course upscale eateries probably won't be interested, and chain restaurants wouldn't either, but family restaurants, cafes, diners, and possibly even bars would gladly accept them.

To find clients to advertise on the placemats, you can send out letters to businesses listed in the telephone book and follow up on the letters with a call or a visit. You may visit restaurants, gas stations, car dealerships, clothing stores, financial institutions, and virtually any other businesses.

The easiest way to coordinate ad space on the placemats may be for you to just print the business cards on the placemats as the ads. You can charge your clients a monthly fee and print out a batch of placemats every month, or you can charge them by the number of placemats on which they wish to place their ad.

Also, don't forget to put your own ad on the placemat so potential clients know how to reach you if they'd like to advertise, too!

What to do with Your Children:
You'll appear more professional if your children don't accompany you when you meet with potential clients. You could meet with clients when your children are at school, being cared for by your spouse, or being supervised by a babysitter. You could also make your telephone calls and go to the printer at those times.

It probably wouldn't hurt for you to bring your children with you when you drop off the placemats, but again, you'd appear more professional if you went alone.

Estimated Time Required:
A meeting with a potential client could take 10-20 minutes, but with established clients, you'll probably just need to call them every month. Dropping off your ads at the printer's, and picking them up, should each only take a few minutes, not counting driving time. Delivering the placemats to restaurants should only take a few minutes, not counting driving time, unless the people there are chatty.

With only about 15 clients, you could probably spend as little as 8 hours per month on this business, but your hours could vary greatly.

Estimated Income:
Your income will depend on the number of clients you have. If you have 15 clients who each pay $50 per month for their ad, you'll earn $750 per month before deducting the cost of the placemats. If you have enough clients to print 2 sets of placemats, with 30 clients total, that would be $1,500 per month before deducting the cost of the placemats.

Of course your rates and income will vary depending on the going rate in your area and the demand for your services.

Estimated Investment Needed:
If you don't charge your clients a deposit before the placemats are printed, you'll have to pay the full cost of printing them out of pocket until you collect the money due to you. If you do charge enough to cover the cost of printing, you shouldn't need to use out-of-pocket money for things other than advertising, telephone calls, and gas for your vehicle.

Advertising:
Word of mouth, mailings, and cold-calling would be best for this business. You could also place an ad in the telephone book.

Additional Information and Resources:
Shop around for printing prices. You could go to Fedex Kinko's or Staples if necessary, but prices at a local printer may be more reasonable.

Postpartum Doula

What You'll Do:
As a postpartum doula, your job will be to assist women after the birth of their child. You'll offer emotional, physical, practical, and informational support. You'll go to your clients' homes and help them during the postpartum period. You may help with laundry, cooking, newborn care, breastfeeding support, emotional support, sibling adjustment, and anything else within the realm of your capabilities. When necessary, you may need to make appropriate referrals, such as for postpartum depression treatment. You won't be a doctor. You'll be a helper.

You'll charge a fee for your services as outlined in the contract that you have your clients sign. You can charge an hourly rate, or you can charge per workday as long as you specify the number of hours your workday will be.

What to do with Your Children:
Your children should definitely not accompany you to work at this job. You could work while your children are at school, or you could leave your children with your husband, another relative, or a babysitter.

Estimated Time Required:
The amount of time you work will depend on the number of clients you have and the amount of help they need. Just figure out how much you want to work and accept clients and refer other clients to other doulas based on that figure.

Estimated Income:
Check around for rates in your area. You can find information online at DONA.org. Then, offer competitive rates. Just as an example though, if you have 2 clients per month and charge each one

$100 per 4-hour workday, and they each utilize your services for 3 days, you'll earn $600 per month.

Estimated Investment Needed:
You may want to check into insurance in case you were to be sued by a client who misunderstood the information you offered, who blamed you for an illness or injury, or just in case you accidentally break something valuable in their home.

You should also be certified. The cost of certification may vary.

Advertising:
I recommend placing and ad in your telephone book. You could also leave flyers and business cards at grocery stores, daycare centers, gyms, doctors' offices, spas, toy stores, hospitals, and birthing centers.

Additional Information and Resources:
For more information, resources, and certification information, visit www.DONA.org.

Potty Training

What You'll Do:
As a professional potty trainer, you'll potty train toddlers. I recommend the book *Potty Training in One Day* by Narmin Parpia. The parents of the children you potty train would have to be willing to follow the routine that you use even when you aren't around, but it is absolutely possible to potty train other people's children. It may take a day, a few days, or even a week, but as long as the toddlers are actually ready to potty train, and you follow the advice in the book, it really can happen.

If you're brave enough, you can conduct this business in your own home. If you think that it would be best for the children to learn in their own home since it's a familiar environment, that's okay, too. I recommend only potty training one child at a time, with the slight exception of twins if they'll cooperate for you.

Since some parents may want to push their child into potty training, you may develop a questionnaire based on the advice in the book to evaluate the toddler's readiness to potty train. Since you may run into this a lot, it may be wise to charge a small screening fee since it will take up a small portion of your time.

The potty training sessions can last for a certain number of hours per day for as many days as it takes for the child to become potty trained. Be sure to give the parents written instructions to follow when you aren't around so the child won't backslide. Since you'll designate a certain number of hours per day to potty train that will be considered one session, you can charge per session since the number of sessions children will need may vary. If the parents aren't helpful in encouraging potty training when the session is over for the day, and the child continually backslides, feel free to drop them as clients until or unless they are ready to be involved in the process.

The parents should provide the training pants or underwear and the extra clothes. If you're potty training the child at their house, the parents should also provide the potty, towels or paper towels for cleaning up accidents, beverages, and food. If you're potty training at your house, and the children don't bring their own potty, you'll need to supply one. You'll also need a drink-and-wet doll, towels or paper towels, beverages, and treats to be used as an incentive. Once the children go home, you'll want to clean up and disinfect everything used for potty training that day.

What to do with Your Children:
Your children would probably just be a distraction to the other children, so if you have very young children, you'll need to have someone else, such as your spouse or a babysitter, care for them. If your children are a bit older, you could work while they're at school.

Estimated Time Required:
The potty training sessions would probably last up to 8 hours per day. If they're too short, they may be ineffective. I wouldn't recommend fewer than 4 hours per day, 6 would be better, and 8 would be great. You would only work with each child for approximately one to five consecutive days before moving on to another client, so the amount of time you'd work per month would depend on the number of children you potty train. Although you could probably potty train full-time, you may work as little as eight or ten hours per week.

As an example, if you did 3 six-hour sessions per week, that would total 18 hours. That's just an example though. Your hours will vary.

Estimated Income:
Your income will depend on the number of clients you have and how long it takes their children to potty train. Your rates will depend on the number of hours a session will last.

For example, if you charged $125 for an 8-hour session, had only one client per week, and potty trained each child in only 2 days, that would put your monthly income at $1,000. If you also charged $25 per potty-training-readiness evaluation, and evaluated 2 children per week, that would add another $200 to your monthly income before any applicable expenses.

Of course the amount you charge will depend on the going rate in your area, but you could probably make a decent income from this no matter where you live.

Estimated Investment Needed:

The first investment you'll make will be to purchase the potty training book. Although you could borrow it from your library, it would be best to have a copy on hand to review if necessary. You may want to purchase a couple extra copies to lend to your clients so they can better understand the process and be more involved.

I recommend that you obtain clearances, and you should definitely keep your CPR and first aid certifications current. If you're potty training the children in your own home, and you don't have your house childproofed, you'll probably want to spend the little bit that it costs to properly childproof.

Other costs may include the purchase of a drink-and-wet doll, a potty, lots of towels or paper towels, treats as incentive for the children, beverages, snacks, and cleaning products.

Advertising:

Word of mouth will be your best advertising for this business. Once you've got one happy client, she'll probably tell numerous other people about your services.

To get started, you could leave business cards and hang flyers at day care centers, pediatricians' offices, family restaurants, toy stores, and grocery stores. People may be skeptical at first, but once you start getting clients, more will likely follow.

Of course telling your supportive friends and neighbors to spread the word would be helpful, too.

Additional Information and Resources:

Potty Training in One Day by Narmin Parpia can be purchased from most book stores. You could also order it, and the drink and wet doll, online from www.Amazon.com.

www.BabyMallOnline.com is an affordable website from which you could purchase a potty or recommend to clients for potty training supplies.

Private Investigating

What You'll Do:
As a private investigator, you'll be hired to perform various investigations. You may track down and adoptee's birth parents, investigate suspicious insurance claims, find evidence of a spouse's infidelity, or investigate other types of cases. You may recover deleted emails, take photographs, videotape subjects, and use various other methods to complete your investigations.

You could investigate for individuals, police departments, insurance companies, or other businesses.

What to do with Your Children:
Your definitely can't bring your children with you for this job, so if your spouse won't be home to watch them, you'll need to have a relative or babysitter care for them. Since the work hours for this job are irregular, your work nights would be great nights for the children to a have a sleepover at their grandmother's house or with another relative. If you're working during the day, perhaps you could do so while your children are at school. When investigating online, you could work while your children are napping or asleep at night.

Estimated Time Required:
The amount of time you'll work will depend on the demand for your services, the complexity of the cases, and the length of time it takes you to complete your investigations. There is no reliable estimate for the amount of time this job would require. It could probably be part-time or full-time. Just accept and decline jobs based on your availability for work.

Estimated Income:
Your income will depend on the number of investigations for which you're hired, but if you charge $15 per hour and work two 8-hour investigations per month, you'll earn $240 per month. Of course

that's just an example though. The rate you charge will probably depend on the going rate in your area, and rates vary greatly across the country.

Estimated Investment Needed:
You may or may not need a license, depending on the state in which you live. The cost for a license varies, but it may range from a 2-figure to a 3-figure fee.

You may want to receive some training. There are various training options with differing fees. If you choose to receive training, you could choose a course that will match your budget.

You also may want to have a camera and a camcorder.

Advertising:
You could place an ad in the telephone book. You could also create a website. I recommend leaving business cards at law offices.

You could also contact your local police department, attorneys, and insurance offices to inquire about the possibility of them utilizing your services.

Additional Information and Resources:
The following resources may contain information that could be helpful to you for this business.
- www.en.wikipedia.org/wiki/Private_investigator
- www.crimetime.com/licensing.htm
- www.pvteye.com/
- www.fabjob.com/PrivateInvestigator.asp
- www.bls.gov/oco/ocos157.htm
- Everything Private Investigation Book: Master the techniques of the pros to examine evidence, trace down people, and discover the truth by Sheila L. Stephens
- Navigating The Legal Minefield of Private Investigations by Ronald M. Hankin
- The Complete Idiot's Guide to Private Investigating, 2nd Edition by Steven Kerry Brown

Private Security Guard

What You'll Do:
As a private security guard, you'll be hired as needed for single events. You'll be there to prevent a possible crime from happening, sometimes by stopping a dispute. Sometimes your presence alone will be enough to deter crime.

You'll wear a uniform or other clothing that makes you stand out and be recognized as a security guard. Depending on the laws regarding certifications and weapons in your state, you may or may not be in possession of things like pepper spray and handcuffs. You will not be a police officer, nor will you have the authority of one.

You could be hired for many events such as public fundraisers and religious events, but private wedding receptions are common locations for private security guards, too.

You'll probably work mostly evenings and weekends, but you may also work other times, too.

What to do with Your Children:
Your definitely can't bring your children with you for this job, so if your spouse won't be home to watch them, you'll need to have a relative or babysitter care for them. Since you'll probably be working late at most events, your work nights would be great nights for the children to a have a sleepover at their grandmother's house or with another relative.

Estimated Time Required:
Since the time required will depend on the demand for your services, there is no reliable estimate for the hours you'll work. If you work only one 4-hour event every week, that would only be 16 hours per month, but that is just an example.

Estimated Income:
    The pay for private security officers varies greatly from state to state, and even from city to city. Your income will depend not only on your rate of pay, but also on the number of events for which you're hired. Just as an example, if you charge $20 per hour and work two 6-hour shifts per month, you'll earn a monthly income of $240.

Estimated Investment Needed:
    You'll probably need to purchase a uniform, or at least some type of clothing, that identifies you as a security guard. Check your local government's laws regarding training and certification requirements, if any, and to find out how much they'll cost.

Advertising:
    You could place an ad in the telephone book. You could also leave business cards at party supply stores, bridal shops, and other relevant locations. Creating a website could be helpful, too.

Additional Information and Resources:
    Check your local government's laws regarding training and certification requirements, if any.
    Books that you may find helpful are listed below.
- Careers in Private Security: How to Get Started, How to Get Ahead by Leigh Wade
- Private Security and the Law by Charles P. Nemeth
- Introduction to Private Security: Theory Meets Practice by Cliff Roberson and Michael Birzer
- Introduction to Private Security by Kären M. Hess
- Protective Security Law by David W Arnold, Bernard J Farber, and Fred E Inbau

Websites that you may find helpful are listed below.
- www.en.wikipedia.org/wiki/Security_guard
- www.crimedoctor.com/security-guards.htm

Real Estate Agent

What You'll Do:
As a real estate agent, you'll help your clients sell their houses, land, or other buildings. You could specialize in residential or commercial real estate, or you could sell both. You'll list properties on your website, put signs on the properties that are for sale, take potential buyers on tours of the properties, and possibly host open-house events.

You'll earn commissions on the properties you sell. You could work for a real estate company, or you could be self-employed. Either way though, you'll need to be licensed.

What to do with Your Children:
Your children should not accompany you to your clients' homes. You could have your spouse, another relative, or a babysitter watch your children while you work. If your children are older, you could work while they are at school, at a play date, or at sports practice. It would seem unprofessional to bring your children with you when you're meeting with clients or potential buyers.

Estimated Time Required:
The time required would depend on the number of properties you have for sale and the number of potential buyers touring the properties. There is no reliable estimate for the time required, and your work hours will vary.

Estimated Income:
There is no reliable estimate for your income. It will depend on the number of properties you sell, the price they sell for, and the percentage you charge for your commission.

Estimated Investment Needed:
You will need to be trained and licensed. You should also purchase insurance. For sale signs will also need to be purchased.

Advertising:

You could advertise in the newspaper and place an ad in the telephone book. You could leave business cards at various businesses, especially where manufactured homes are sold. A website is practically a must for this business.

You could also contact financial institutions to inquire about selling their foreclosures for them.

Additional Information and Resources:

Check the laws, rules, and regulations of real estate sales before starting this business to make sure you'll be fully prepared and legally compliant.

Some resources that you may find helpful for this business are listed below.

- www.en.wikipedia.org/wiki/Real_estate_agent
- www.fabjob.com/RealEstateAgent.asp
- How to Become a Million Dollar Real Estate Agent in Your First Year: What Smart Agents Need to Know Explained Simply by Susan Smith Alvis and Marie Lujanac
- Success as a Real Estate Agent For Dummies by Dirk Zeller
- SHIFT: How Top Real Estate Agents Tackle Tough Times by Gary Keller
- Your First Year in Real Estate: Making the Transition from Total Novice to Successful Professional by Dirk Zeller

Real Estate Appraisals

What You'll Do:
As a real estate appraiser, you'll determine a property's value based on its market value. You'll tour the property, take photos, ask questions about it, measure it if the measurements aren't already available to you, and research the market value.

You services will probably mostly be used by people who are buying or selling real estate, or by mortgagors.

You'll probably charge a set rate based on the size and/or type of property you're surveying. You may or may not charge different prices for commercial properties than for residential properties, but the prices will probably be based on the size of the property, with commercial buildings usually being larger than residential ones and requiring more measurements to be taken.

What to do with Your Children:
Your children should not accompany you to your clients' properties. You could have your spouse, another relative, or a babysitter watch your children while you work. If your children are older, you could work while they are at school, at a play date, or at sports practice. It would seem unprofessional to bring your children with you when you're meeting with clients.

Estimated Time Required:
The time required would depend on the demand for your services. There is no reliable estimate for the time required, and your work hours will vary.

Estimated Income:
There is no reliable estimate for your income. It will depend on the demand for your services.

Estimated Investment Needed:
You will probably need to be certified or licensed, with the fees and requirements for that varying by location. You should also have a camera for taking photos, and you'll need transportation to get to the properties you're appraising. You should also have a computer with internet access for researching market values, and a tape measure for taking measurements of the properties.

Advertising:
You could advertise in the newspaper and place an ad in the telephone book. You could also leave business cards at various businesses, especially where manufactured homes are sold.
You could also contact financial institutions and realtors to inquire about doing their appraisals on their clients' properties for them.

Additional Information and Resources:
Check the laws, rules, and regulations of real estate appraisals before starting this business to make sure you'll be fully prepared and legally compliant.
Some resources that you may find helpful for this business are listed below.
- www.en.wikipedia.org/wiki/Real_estate_appraisal
- www.appraisalfoundation.org/s_appraisal/index.asp
- www.bls.gov/oco/ocos300.htm
- www.orea.ca.gov
- The Art of Real Estate Appraisal: The Complete Guide for Homeowners and Real Estate Professionals by William Ventolo and Martha R. Williams
- How to Get Started in the Real Estate Appraisal Business by Dan Nahorney and Vicki Lankarge

Rental Properties

What You'll Do:

This could be an easy way to make some extra money with very minimal effort, assuming the residence you rent is in good condition and requires minimal, if any, ongoing repairs. As a landlord, you'll rent out a residence to a tenant, or multiple residences to multiple tenants if you can.

So, where are you going to find a residence to put up for rent? You could rent out your garage apartment if you have one. You could purchase a mobile home and place it on vacant land that you own or even in a mobile home park. If you place it in a mobile home park, you'll pay to rent the lot that it's on, but you can still rent the residence to a tenant. If you could afford the investment, you could purchase a foreclosed home or apartment complex as an investment property. You could even rent out a building you may have that would be a suitable location for a business.

Once you've got a residence to rent out, and potential renters are interested, you'll check their references and run a background check on them. After all, you probably don't want to rent to someone who may not pay you or who will damage the property. Once you've found a suitable renter, you'll have them sign a rental agreement.

You could have a lawyer draw up a rental agreement for you, or you could find them online. Make sure it specifies whether or not pets are allowed and all other pertinent information, including who handles improvements and repairs. You'll collect a security deposit, usually the amount of one month's rent, when the agreement is signed.

The renters will send you a check every month for the rent that they owe you. If they miss a payment, you evict them and rent to someone else.

You could also rent out commercial properties or storage rental units.

What to do with Your Children:
Your time with your children shouldn't be affected much by this business. You may have to answer a few phone calls and meet with potential renters to have them tour the residence and sign the rental agreement, but once you have a renter, you won't have to show the residence until or unless those renters decide to move out.

If you wanted to take your children with you when you show the residence to potential renters, you could. If not, you could go while they're at school or while your spouse is home to watch them.

Estimated Time Required:
Once the residence is rented, you may only need a couple minutes to answer the phone every so often if your renter has any questions. If any repairs are needed, you may have to call a repairman, but you could state in your rental agreement that your renter must coordinate repairs.

Estimated Income:
The amount you charge for the monthly rental will depend on the area in which you live, the size of the residence, and the type of residence. Houses would probably bring in more rent than mobile homes or apartments. Buildings used for businesses would probably earn you more money that buildings used as residences. Just check out the "real estate for rent" section of your newspaper to see what others are charging. That'll give you an idea of how much you could earn from your rental. Of course if you still have a mortgage out on the residence, your income will be less than you charge for rent, but if you put the extra income toward the mortgage, you could pay it off much earlier.

Estimated Investment Needed:
If you already own the residence, the initial investment should be minimal, if one is even required. If you need to buy a residence to rent, you'll probably need to take out a loan for that, and you'd want to purchase homeowners insurance. You'll also be responsible for the property taxes. The amount of the loan would depend on the cost of real estate in your area.

Advertising:
You could place a "for rent" sign at the residence or put an ad in your local newspaper. You could also hang flyers at virtually any business, perhaps even at a real estate office.

Additional Information and Resources:
Don't forget to check with your local governing authority for laws, rules, and regulations, and for possible building permits you may need.

Restaurant Dessert Baking

What You'll Do:
      To get started as a restaurant dessert baker, you will contact one or more restaurants in your area and inquire about them selling your homemade desserts in their restaurant. You can provide them with samples and allow them to choose which desserts they would like to offer in their restaurant and how many they would like to purchase each week.
      Once you and the owners reach an agreement, you make the homemade desserts at your house in your own kitchen and deliver them to the restaurant on the specified days each week.
      Most restaurants offer fruit pies and cream pies. Some offer cakes, cookies, donuts, cream horns, éclairs, and cheesecake. You will sell whole desserts, but the restaurants will sell the whole desserts in single servings, such as a slice of pie.
      Once the desserts are made, be sure to package them carefully, label each box or container with the name of the dessert and the date it was made. Deliver them to the restaurant, and collect your money!

What to do with Your Children:
      Young children usually like to help out in the kitchen, so you may be able to keep them entertained by letting them stir pudding and frosting. Letting them help will almost certainly slow you down and create a bigger mess, but at least you'll get to spend time with them! You can do the decorating or any intricate details on the desserts while they nap or watch a favorite television show. If you can't leave them at home with your husband or someone else, make sure the desserts are kept in the trunk of your car on the drive to the restaurant to deliver them. You wouldn't want a toy flying out of your child's hand to land on top of a lemon meringue pie! Even if it's in a bakery box, the meringue would still almost certainly be ruined.
      If your children are older, you could get your baking done while they're at school and deliver the desserts just before you pick

them up at the end of the school day. During summer break, they could either help you or keep themselves entertained for a short period while you bake. They could ride along in the car with you when you deliver the desserts, too.

Estimated Time Required:
It would probably take around an hour to make a pie. You could double or triple the recipes to make 2 or 3 in an hour. You'll have time while they're baking to begin another dessert. Cakes may take 45-60 minutes, plus time to cool and time to decorate them. More delicate desserts and single-serving desserts may take longer.

The time you devote to this business will depend on the number of desserts you're making per week.

Estimated Income:
The going rate for whole desserts will probably vary by location. Contact a local company that sells factory-made desserts for restaurant sales to see what they charge, and then offer the restaurants a competitive price.

Although prices will vary, if it costs you $5 to make a pie, you sell each pie for $10, and you sell 20 pies per week, you'll net $100 per week for total monthly income of around $400. That's just an example though. Your income will vary.

Estimated Investment Needed:
You will need to purchase ingredients to make the desserts, pie tins, and bakery boxes. You'll be responsible for the increased gas or electric bill from the oven to bake your desserts.

If you don't already have enough mixing bowls, kitchen utensils, and other kitchen items needed, you'll have to buy those, too.

If any licenses, permits, or other regulatory standards are needed, you will also be responsible for those fees.

Advertising:
You could send brochures and business cards to restaurants that you'd like to provide desserts for, but talking to the owners face-to-face would probably get you a more favorable response. Bring samples, and possibly photos, of desserts you can make to the restaurants. Word of mouth would be great, too.

Your desserts will probably be advertised on the menu in the restaurants that serve them.

Additional Information and Resources:
Check with your local government office to find out the rules and regulations regarding food sales and home baking businesses in your area. Your kitchen may need to be inspected to make sure it's a sanitary environment. You may need a license or permit, and you may need to register your business.

Resume Writing

What You'll Do:
As a resume writer, you'll meet with clients and gather information about their work experience, qualifications, and any special skills or training they may possess. They may already have a resume. If they do, that makes your job easier. You'll be able to rewrite their resume and improve upon it. If they don't already have a resume, you'll create one for them based on the information with which they provide you.

Virtually anyone could be a resume writer. After obtaining the information necessary from your client, you just type up a summary of the information you've been given. Generally, you'll probably receive a fixed payment per resume, but for clients who require a great deal of your time, you may charge an hourly rate instead. You should receive your payment in full at the time you give the completed resumes to your clients.

What to do with Your Children:
Do not bring your children with you when meeting your clients face-to-face. Instead, you could meet with them while your children are at school, sports, or grandma's house. You could also meet with clients at times when your husband would be home to watch the children.

If you're gathering information from a client over the telephone or via email, you can do that in the comfort of your home while your children are napping, playing quietly, or watching television.

You can use any uninterrupted time you have to type up the resumes. You could type them while your children are napping, at school, or while your husband is playing with them.

You can fax, email, hand-deliver, or have the resumes picked up from your house. All but the delivery method would not require you to have someone else supervise your children. If you're delivering the resumes to a client's home or meeting a client elsewhere, you'll want to do so without your children.

Estimated Time Required:

A fair estimate would be that you'll spend 2-3 hours total per client. Gathering information may take an hour. Creating the resume may take an hour. Meeting to deliver the resume may take up to an hour depending on how far away from home you have to go to deliver it. That's just an estimate though. Your hours will vary by client.

Estimated Income:

The amount you charge for the resume will depend on the going rate in your area. If jobs are in high demand, you'll likely be able to charge more than you would if the job market was stable.

You will probably charge a minimum of $25 per resume, but may be able to charge as much as $125 if there's a great demand for your service.

Of course your income will depend on the number of clients you have, but if you charge $45 per resume and have 2 clients per week, you'd earn $360 per month. That's just an example though. Your income will vary.

Estimated Investment Needed:

The initial investment needed would mainly be for the cost of advertising. Other than that, you'll need a telephone, a computer, and a printer.

If you'd like to research resume writing, you can check out books at your local library rather than buying them. If you choose to pay for a resume writing course or instructions, at the time of this writing, www.MyResumeBiz.com has a program for $99, but it may or may not be necessary for this business.

Advertising:

I would suggest hanging flyers, especially near unemployment offices. You could leave business cards on bulletin boards anywhere. I would also recommend placing an ad in your newspaper. Most people looking for work search the classifieds section of newspapers for jobs, so your ad would likely attract attention.

Additional Information and Resources:

MyResumeBiz.com offers a resume writing business program. Some books that may be helpful to you include:

- Blue Collar & Beyond: Resumes for Skilled Trades & Services by Yana Parker
- *Resume Magic: Trade Secrets of a Professional Resume Writer* by Susan Britton Whitcomb
- The Resume.com Guide to Writing Unbeatable Resumes by Warren Simons and Rose Curtis
- *Amazing Resumes: What Employers Want to See—and How to Say It* by Jim, Ph.D. Bright and Joanne, Ph.D. Earl
- *How to Say It on Your Resume: A Top Recruiting Director's Guide to Writing the Perfect Resume for Every Job* by Brad Karsh with Courtney Pike

Reupholstery

What You'll Do:
When reupholstering, you'll replace the current fabric coverings attached to various pieces of furniture with new fabric coverings. You'll remove the old and put on the new.

Your customers will generally have their furniture reupholstered because the fabric covering has become torn, stained, or otherwise damaged. Sometimes people have their furniture reupholstered just because they want a new texture, design, or color scheme. It's generally less expensive to have furniture reupholstered than it is to buy new furniture.

You could provide swatches of fabric that you could purchase yourself for customers to choose from, or you could have your customers provide their own fabric.

Since furniture can be large and take up alot of space, you'll probably need an empty room at your house in which to work. If you don't have the extra room at your house, you could always go to your customers' homes to work.

What to do with Your Children:
You definitely don't want your children to damage the new fabric or injure themselves with a staple gun, so if you're working at home, you should probably work while your children are napping, at school, or being supervised by someone else.

If you're going to your customers' homes, you'll need to leave your children with your husband or another responsible caregiver, or you could go while your children are at school.

Estimated Time Required:
The amount of time you spend working will depend on the size of the furniture, the complexity of attaching the new fabric, your speed at attaching the new fabric, and the number of reupholstering jobs you have. It probably won't be full-time unless you want it to

be, so accept, decline, and postpone jobs based on the amount of time you want to spend working.

Estimated Income:
Your income will depend on the number of reupholstering jobs you have and how much you charge for your services. The going rate for reupholstering will vary by location, so check around for prices in your area and offer a competitive rate.

Just as an example though, if you charge $250 per couch, not counting the cost of materials, and you reupholster 1 couch every 2 weeks, you'd earn $500 per month.

Decide how much you want to earn, set your prices, and accept and decline jobs based on your desired income.

Estimated Investment Needed:
You may or may not want to offer fabric swatches for customers to choose from. If you're providing the new fabric, you'll need to purchase it yourself, but you should obtain a deposit from your customers beforehand. Other than that, you'll need a staple gun, staples, and scissors. You may need other tools to remove the old fabric and the old staples.

Advertising:
You could advertise in the newspaper and telephone book. You could also hang flyers or leave business cards at craft supply stores, furniture stores, home improvement stores, and other stores that may have customers that would be interested in your services.

Word of mouth would be great advertising, especially if it came from a happy customer.

Additional Information and Resources:
Some websites you may find helpful for this business are listed below.
- www.repair-home.com/how_to_reupholster_furniture.html
- www.wikihow.com/Reupholster-a-Couch
- www.youtube.com/watch?v=GIcq_qq3m7c
- www.upholster.com

Sewing

What You'll Do:

As a seamstress, you'll mend clothing, perform alterations, sew on patches, and possibly even make clothing, pillows, and curtains. Though making wedding dresses from scratch probably won't be your main business, if you want to offer that service, go for it!

This would be a great business if you live near a military base, a prison, or anywhere else that has a large number of employees that are required to wear uniforms.

You could choose to specialize and offer only alterations, only sewing on patches, or whatever it is you want to do, but you'll probably have more business if you offer many services.

Your customers will drop the clothing off at your house. If alterations are being done, you'll need to measure a pin the fabric in place. You'll perform the sewing that your customers desire, either by hand or using a sewing machine. The customers will pick up their items from you and pay you for your services.

If you're doing alterations, you'll need a private room for your customers to try on the clothing for you to measure it. You could offer them the bathroom, a guest bedroom, or your sewing room for that.

What to do with Your Children:

Your children might be a distraction to you if they're in the room while you're measuring, but you could set up your sewing machine in the living room to be near them while you work if you want. Any project requiring great concentration and intricate detail could be done while the kids are sleeping, at school, or being supervised by your spouse or another relative.

Estimated Time Required:

The time required would depend on how fast you sew, the number of customers you have, the intricacy of the projects, and whether you sew by hand or with a sewing machine. There is no reliable estimate for the amount of time you'd work. Just take on as many or as few projects as you're comfortable with, and after a while you'll be able to judge how long a project will take you to complete.

Estimated Income:
　　　　Your income will depend on the number of customers you have and how much you charge for your various sewing services. You may charge set rates for hemming pants, sewing on buttons, replacing zippers, sewing on patches, and other services. There is no reliable estimate of income from this job.

Estimated Investment Needed:
　　　　You would need needles, thread, and scissors, and possibly a measuring tape, pins, thimbles, buttons, zippers, fabric, and seam-rippers. If you want to use a sewing machine but don't have one, of course you'd need to buy one.

Advertising:
　　　　Word of mouth will be good advertising. Happy customers will probably tell others about your services. You could also place an ad in the newspaper and telephone book, but flyers would probably be cheaper. You could hang flyers at grocery stores, laundromats, and other businesses.

Additional Information and Resources:
　　　　You can compare prices online and order a sewing machine at www.Amazon.com or various other retailers. You could also look online at www.Overstock.com.

Snow Removal

What You'll Do:

For snow removal, you'll use a shovel, a snow blower, or a snowplow that is attached to the front of your vehicle to remove snow. You could perform snow removal services for individuals or businesses. You may shovels sidewalks, plow parking lots and driveways, or use a snow blower to remove snow from sidewalks and driveways. Although this is just a seasonal job, it could be lucrative in the busy months.

What to do with Your Children:

Since you'll be performing snow removal in the winter, most of the time that you work may be when your children are at school. On the weekends and over Christmas break, if your children are old enough, you could allow them to help you shovel. If you're using a vehicle to plow snow, your children could ride along.

If you'll be performing snow removal when your children aren't in school, or if your children are too young for school and you can't bring them with you, you could leave them with your husband, a babysitter, or another qualified caregiver.

Estimated Time Required:

The time you spend on snow removal will depend on the demand for your services, the size of the area from which the snow needs to be removed, and your method of snow removal. The hours you work will probably vary from day to day during the winter months. This is a seasonal job that will have more of a demand the farther north you live.

Estimated Income:

Your rates will depend on the method of snow removal you're using, your rates, and the demand for your services. Check the going rate for snow removal in your area, and offer competitive rates.

Estimated Investment Needed:
You'll need a shovel, a snow blower, or a vehicle with a plow. For a snow blower or vehicle, you'll also need fuel. For a vehicle, you'll also need vehicle insurance.

Advertising:
Hang flyers and/or leave business cards at virtually any business. You could place an ad in the newspaper and telephone book. You could even put a magnetic sign on your vehicle.

Additional Information and Resources:
If you're plowing snow, you may want to check with your insurance company to see if your policy covers using your vehicle for business purposes.
If you wanted to, you could also offer to treat surfaces with anti-skid or salt.

Stand-up Comedy

What You'll Do:
    As a stand-up comic, you'll entertain audiences with your comedy act. You could tell jokes, point out obviously funny cultural trends or perspectives, tell funny stories, or use some other means of providing humor.
    You'll probably work mostly weekend evenings, but you may also work other times, too.

What to do with Your Children:
    You won't be bringing your children with you for this job unless they're old enough, you're working at a public rather than private event, your comedy is age-appropriate for them, you're working in a child-friendly environment, and another caregiver comes along to supervise them while you work.
    You'll probably leave your children at home with your husband, but if your husband won't be home to watch them, you'll need to have a relative or babysitter care for them. Since you may be working late, your work nights would be great nights for the children to a have a sleepover at their grandmother's house or with another relative.

Estimated Time Required:
    You'll probably be working mostly Friday and Saturday nights, but how often you work will depend on the demand for your comedy act, so your hours will vary. Just as an example though, if you work only one hour every Saturday night, that would only be 4 hours per month.

Estimated Income:
    Your income will depend on how often your act is booked and the amount the location pays its entertainers. Since it could vary so greatly, there is no reliable estimate of income for this job.

Estimated Investment Needed:
There's no mandatory investment for this job, but you could buy a few books on the subject if you wanted to.

Advertising:
I recommend approaching the managers, or whoever is in charge of booking the entertainment, at clubs, hotels, bars, and lounges to inquire about the possibility of them booking your act at their business. Other than that, you could place an ad in the telephone book and leave business cards at random places. Since various events book entertainment, you could leave business cards at restaurants and other places that may have banquet halls.

Additional Information and Resources:
The following resources may include information that you may find helpful for this job.
- www.fabjob.com/Comic.asp
- Step by Step to Stand-Up Comedy by Greg Dean
- Getting the Joke: The Inner Workings of Stand-Up Comedy by Oliver Double
- Teach Yourself Stand-Up Comedy by Logan Murray
- Comedy FAQs and Answers: How the Stand-up Biz Really Works by Dave Schwensen

Tanning Salon

What You'll Do:

If you have a free room in your house or can covert your garage, you could open a tanning salon. Unlike hair salons, to the best of my knowledge, you currently don't need to be a licensed professional to operate a tanning salon, but you may still need to register your business and apply for any necessary permits.

Many people own tanning beds for personal use. You would simply own tanning beds that customers could use, and charge them a fee for using them. Don't forget to sanitize the tanning beds and make sure they're properly maintained.

Have each client sign a waiver or release, and make sure they wear protective glasses made specifically for tanning bed use. Then show them how to use the tanning beds, and allow them to tan for the amount of time for which they've paid.

Other than cleaning the tanning beds, this income stream is fairly hands-off.

What to do with Your Children:

Since your clients will probably be unsupervised while they're tanning, just keep your children out of the room where the tanning beds are while your clients are tanning.

Estimated Time Required:

You will generally need to show most clients how to use the tanning beds only on their first visit. You can wipe down the tanning beds in just a few minutes after each client is done. Some salons leave a stack of towels and a spray bottle of disinfectant for each client to clean the tanning bed before and after they use it, too. Just to be sure the tanning beds are being cleaned though, you should probably clean them yourself even if you leave cleaners for your clients.

If there's no timer in the salon, you'll need to alert your clients when their session is over.

You will probably only spend a few minutes in the salon per client that comes each day. You can set the business hours to times that work well for you and maybe even allow yourself a day off.

You could probably devote no more than an hour per day to this mostly hands-off business, but your hours will vary.

Estimated Income:

Check your area for local rates. Set a competitive price. You could charge people per session (10, 15, etc. minutes), per week, or per month. Your price and the number of clients you have will determine your income.

Estimated Investment Needed:

You'll need a room in which to put the tanning beds, tanning beds, towels and sanitizer. You should have a pair of glasses made specifically for tanning bed use for clients to use in case they forget to bring their own. You'll also be responsible for maintenance of the tanning beds, the cost of new bulbs when needed, and the cost of electricity used to operate the tanning beds.

Advertising:

You could hang flyers on local bulletin boards and in the windows of hair and nail salons. Newspaper advertising and an ad in the telephone book would also be helpful. Word of mouth would be greatly beneficial, too.

Additional Information and Resources:

Compare tanning bed prices and ratings to determine which ones would be best for your business. An internet search engine could be helpful for that.

The Stock Market

What You'll Do:

Stock market investing could be profitable. It could also be risky. With that said, there's more than one way to make money in the stock market.

You could buy stocks and sell them when the price goes up. You could buy and hold stocks for their dividends. You could buy or sell stock options, which are like bets as to whether a certain stock's value will increase or decrease.

You could set up an online investment account and manage your own transactions, or you could invest through a stock broker.

What to do with Your Children:

You could conduct your research of stocks while your children are napping, at school, at sports practice, or are being supervised by your husband. You could also make your online transactions then, or call your stock broker at those times, too.

Estimated Time Required:

The time you spend on this income stream will depend on the amount of research you conduct and the number of transactions you make. You could definitely do this part-time, but there's no reliable way to estimate the time required without knowing the two factors listed above.

Estimated Income:

The amount of income you earn will depend on the amount of money you invest, any dividends you may earn, how much the stock prices increase or decrease, the transaction fees, and any applicable taxes. Without knowing those factors, there's no reliable estimate of income for this income stream.

Estimated Investment Needed:
You'll need money for your initial investment in the stocks or options. You may also need to pay transaction fees.

Advertising:
You won't advertise. You'll just research stocks and make purchases and sales.

Additional Information and Resources:
Make sure to keep a record of your transactions. You'll need that information for tax purposes.

The following resources may contain information that could be helpful for this income stream.

- www.investopedia.com/articles/optioninvestor/03/073003.asp
- www.Scottrade.com
- www.RJOfutures.com
- www.ehow.com/how_2075625_day-trade-stock-options.html
- www.stocks.about.com/od/advancedtrading/a/Optitrad031005.htm
- Understanding Options by Michael Sincere
- The Rookie's Guide to Options: The Beginner's Handbook of Trading Equity Options by Mark D. Wolfinger
- Trading Stock Options: Basic Option Trading Strategies And How I've Used Them To Profit In Any Market by Brian Burns
- Options for the Beginner and Beyond: Unlock the Opportunities and Minimize the Risks by W. Edward Olmstead
- The Complete Guide to Investing in Short Term Trading: How to Earn High Rates of Returns Safely by Alan Northcott
- Trend Trading for a Living: Learn the Skills and Gain the Confidence to Trade for a Living by Thomas K. Carr
- How to Make Money in Stocks: A Winning System in Good Times and Bad, Fourth Edition by William J. O'Neil
- Trading For Dummies by Michael Griffis and Lita Epstein

Translating

What You'll Do:
As a translator, your job will be to convert, or translate, written words from one language into another. You'll need to know more than the technical terminology of the words though. You'll also need to understand the language well enough to know when to metaphrase and when to paraphrase.

You may translate documents, web pages, or even entire books. You could translate for schools, publishing companies, internet marketers, or even a translating agency.

When taking on jobs, though, remember that it's easier to translate into your native language than it is to translate your native language into another language.

What to do with Your Children:
Even though you'll most likely be working from home, you'll still need to find time to work when your children won't interrupt you. You could try to do most of your translating while your children are at school, at sports practice, at a playdate, or at a relative's house. You could also hire a babysitter to care for your children while you work, or you could have your husband supervise them for a while.

Estimated Time Required:
The time you spend working will depend on the demand for your services and the amount of material each job requires you to translate. Your schedule will probably vary. You'll probably work on an as-needed basis.

To be in control of your schedule, decide how much time you want to spend working, and accept and decline jobs based on that.

Estimated Income:
At the time of this writing, you could probably earn anywhere from $12 to $30 per hour, or more, depending on your experience. Your income would be difficult to estimate beforehand without

knowing the demand for your service. If you spend 4 hours translating one document two times per month, at a rate of $25 per hour, you'd earn $200 per month. That's just an example though. Your income will vary.

Estimated Investment Needed:
The investment for this job will depend on the languages you currently speak. If English is your only language, you'll definitely need to receive formal training in another language. I believe license and certification requirements vary by state.

You'll also probably need a dictionary, a computer with internet access, a phone, and possibly a fax machine.

Advertising:
You could send business cards and letters explaining your services to schools, colleges, universities, various types of corporations, publishing companies, and other businesses. You could also place an ad in telephone books.

Since translating jobs can be done long distance, you could create a website and/or advertise online. You could also search for jobs online at freelance websites.

Additional Information and Resources:
The following resources may have information that could be helpful for this job.
- www.translation-and-languages.com
- www.collegegrad.com/careers/proft105.shtml
- www.atanet.org/
- www.en.wikipedia.org/wiki/Translation
- How to Succeed as a Freelance Translator *by* Corinne McKay
- A Practical Guide for Translators (Topics in Translation) by Geoffrey Samuelsson-Brown
- Becoming a Translator: An Introduction to the Theory and Practice of Translation by Douglas Robinson
- Language into Language: Cultural, Legal and Linguistic Issues for Interpreters and Translators by Saul Sibirsky and Martin C. Taylor

Travel Agent

What You'll Do:
     As a travel agent, your job will be to sell travel-related products and services. A travel agent could also be referred to as a travel consultant because you'll consult with your customers about their desired trips. You'll probably earn commission from airlines, hotels, and other such companies when you sell their products and/or services. If the businesses don't offer you a commission, you'll have to charge a fee on top of the prices being charged as your source of income.
     You'll make airline reservations, book hotel rooms, provide itineraries, and offer suggestions to your customers. They'll tell you what they want and you'll make all of the necessary arrangements for it to happen.
     You could make travel arrangements for all types of trips, or you could specialize in business trips, cruises, honeymoons, family vacations, or some other type of travel.
     Although some travel agents are employees of travel agencies, you could be an independent travel agent, or you could start your own travel agency.

What to do with Your Children:
     Your children should not be present when you're meeting with clients or conversing on the telephone. You could try to do most of your work while your children are at school, at a playdate, at sports practice, or napping. You could also have your husband, a babysitter, or another relative supervise your children for you while you work. If your children are adolescents, they should be able to read a book, watch television, or do some other solo activity while you are in another room on the telephone or at the computer making reservations.

Estimated Time Required:

The time you spend working will depend on the demand for your services and the types of trips you're booking. Unless you're the travel agent for a large company that requires their employees to travel frequently, you probably won't work full-time.

Estimated Income:

Your commission would probably be in the ballpark of 8-10% of your sales. Your income will depend on the number of sales you make, and the price of each one.

Just as an example, if you sell just one $3,500 cruise per month, at 10% commission, you'd earn a monthly commission of $350. Of course, your income will vary.

Estimated Investment Needed:

You may or may not need to be licensed, depending on your state's laws regarding travel.

You could invest in travel and tourism training. That could probably range from a few hundred dollars to many thousands of dollars.

Other than that, you'll need a telephone and a computer with internet access. If you're meeting with clients face-to-face, you'll probably need an office, or you could meet your clients at a restaurant, at their home or office, or at some other location.

Advertising:

I highly recommend placing and ad in your telephone book. Since travel planning can be done over the telephone, you could also create a website and register your business on online search engines to reach potential clients hundreds and even thousands of miles away. You could also place an ad in the newspaper, rent a billboard, pay for radio or television advertisements, and leave business cards at various locations.

If you're specializing in business trips, you could send business cards, brochures, and letters detailing your services to various businesses for which you'd like to coordinate travel.

Additional Information and Resources:

The following resources may contain information that you may find helpful for this business.
- www.pennfoster.edu/travel/index.html
- www.fabjob.com/travelconsultant.asp
- www.en.wikipedia.org/wiki/Travel_agency
- www.careeroverview.com/travel-agent-careers.html
- www.careeroverview.com/travel-agent-careers.html
- Home-Based Travel Agent, 5th Edition by Kelly Monaghan
- Design and Launch an Online Travel Business in a Week by Charlene Davis
- How to Start a Home Based Travel Agency Independent Study Course by Tom Ogg and Joanie Ogg
- Travel Planning Online for Dummies by Noah Vadnai and Julian Smith

Tutoring

What You'll Do:

As a tutor, you'll be like an after-school teacher. You'll try to teach children the things that they're having trouble learning in school. It may be algebra, trigonometry, reading, spelling, history, foreign language, music, or even home economics. It will depend on the ages of the children you tutor and their strengths and weaknesses.

Some children need more one-on-one time with an educator than their teachers in school can give them. Those children need tutors. Tutors can review the lessons taught in school that day, help with homework, or create their own lesson plan that fits with what the children are supposed to be learning in school.

You'll only tutor children in the subjects in which you're proficient, so you won't need to learn anything you don't already know, unless you'd like to. You'll tutor children during your chosen hours after school, on weekends, during the summer, over holiday breaks, or any combination of those times.

What to do with Your Children:

I suggest one-on-one time with the children you're tutoring. If they're in the same classes as your children, they may feel embarrassed about being in the presence of fellow classmates while being tutored, especially if your children understand the lessons better than they do. You may want to tutor the children while your children are at a friend or relative's house. You could tutor the children while your children are at a playdate or while your husband takes them for a walk or to the park. You could also tutor the children while your children are at sports practice, drama club meetings, or some other activity.

Estimated Time Required:

Tutoring sessions generally last one hour a day, one to three days a week. Some children need more help and could be tutored every day after school.

The time you spend tutoring depends on how many children you choose to tutor and how much help they need. If you tutor just two children three days out of the week, that would only be six hours. Just decide how much time you want to spend tutoring, and accept or decline students based on that.

Estimated Income:

Hourly rates vary by area, but it would probably be safe to assume you could charge at least $10 - $12 per hour per child in most areas. If you have a teaching degree, you will probably earn more.

Estimated Investment Needed:

There's probably no mandatory investment, but you may want to obtain clearances. You'll probably only need things you already have around your house, like pencils, paper, a calculator, and other miscellaneous items.

Advertising:

Tell your friends, neighbors, and fellow parents. If you know the teachers and faculty at your child's school well, ask them to recommend you to other parents. Word of mouth is great advertising for tutoring. You could also place an ad in your local newspaper and hang a flyer on the school's bulletin board.

Additional Information and Resources:

You may want to consider obtaining clearances. That's always a good idea for businesses in which you'll be working with children.

Also, don't advertise as a teacher unless you have a teaching degree. Tutors don't necessarily need a degree.

Vehicle Detailing

What You'll Do:

As a vehicle detailer, you'll clean practically every inch of the vehicles that you're detailing. From the stereo buttons and automatic lock buttons to the tires and rims, you'll carefully clean it all.

You could do this as your own business, or you could try to contract with a vehicle repair shop or car dealership, or even multiple repair shops and dealerships. Then, whenever they get a vehicle in that will need detailed, they'll give you a call. If you're detailing for another business, they'll be the ones to pay you. If you're detailing as a private detailer, the owners of the vehicles will pay you.

You'll probably charge a fixed rate price rather than an hourly rate, and you'll probably have a different fee for cars than trucks because the size difference will affect the time you'll spend detailing.

If you're operating as a private business, your customers will probably bring their vehicles to you. If you're detailing for another business, you'll probably have to go to that business.

What to do with Your Children:

If you're detailing as a private business, you can detail the vehicles while your children are napping if you've got a baby monitor to take outside or into your garage with you. You could also work while they're at school or while your husband or other relative is taking care of them.

If you're detailing for another business, you can work while your children are at school or sports practice, at a playdate, or are being cared for by your spouse or another relative. You could also hire a babysitter if you'd like.

Estimated Time Required:

The size of the vehicle, the amount of filth it has accumulated, and the speed at which you clean will determine the amount of time you'll spend detailing. Because trucks are bigger, they will generally take longer to detail than cars.

It may take you 2 hours. It may take you 4 hours. I recommend detailing your own vehicle for practice to give you an idea of how long it may take.

Of course the number of vehicles available for you to detail will determine how many hours you work per week, but you could decline jobs if necessary if you find yourself working more than you'd like.

Estimated Income:

Your income will depend on the number of vehicles you detail, but it should be safe to assume that you could charge at least $45 per car and $50 per truck. You could probably charge more. At those rates though, you could easily make around $400 per month, before deducting the cost of the cleaning products used, by detailing only 2 vehicles per week.

Estimated Investment Needed:

You would need to buy cleaning products such as glass cleaner and other cleaners that would be available in the car care section of stores. Although you could buy cleaning cloths, you may be able to use old t-shirts or other clothing instead.

Advertising:

Hanging flyers and leaving business cards at car dealerships and repair shops would be great advertising. You could also put an ad in your local newspaper and telephone book directory.

Additional Information and Resources:

To check into car care products, the following websites may be helpful to you.
- www.premiumautocare.com
- www.autogeek.net
- www.meguiars.com

<u>Videography</u>

What You'll Do:
    As a videographer, you'll simply record events with a video camera. After recording the event, or parts of the event, you'll most likely edit your footage. You may leave the footage unedited at times when you and your clients agree to do so, but that would mainly be when you record short events or only parts of events.
    You could contract to record special events such as weddings, graduations, and other special ceremonies. You could record footage for documentaries. You could even record footage for various types of training videos. Although those are all possibilities, the majority of your work will probably be done at weddings.
    The finished video will most likely be delivered as a DVD, but it may be delivered on a VHS tape as long as your clients consent to that ahead of time.

What to do with Your Children:
    If you need uninterrupted time to edit the videos, you could have your husband care for your children, or you could hire a babysitter to supervise them while you work at your computer.
    When you have to leave the house to go to the event, you'll need to go while your children are being supervised by your husband, a babysitter, or another qualified caregiver.

Estimated Time Required:
    The time required will depend on the number of clients you have and the types of events you're recording. If the contract states the amount of hours you'll work instead of just that you'll record the event, you'll have a much better idea of how much time you'll spend working. Since the jobs and contracts can vary, there is no reliable estimate for the time required. To be in control of your schedule, accept and decline jobs based on the amount of time you have available to work.

Estimated Income:

The rates of videographers vary greatly, and business varies by season. Check around for other videographers' rates in your area, and charge a competitive price.

Just as an example though, if you record a wedding every other week, at a flat fee of $500, you'd have a monthly income of $1,000. That's just an example though. Your income will vary.

Estimated Investment Needed:

You'll definitely need a video camera for this job. You may also need extra storage for your digital video camera. To edit the videos, you'll need a computer. You'll also need blank DVDs on which the event will be put to be given to your clients.

Advertising:

You could place an ad in the telephone book and newspaper. You could leave business cards at bridal shops, party supply stores, and other relevant locations. Additionally, you could set up a website that displays your contact information.

Additional Information and Resources:

You may want to check into your copyright rights.

Some websites that you may find helpful for this business are listed below.
- www.wedplan.net/videographers
- www.copyright.gov/help/faq/faq-fairuse.html
- www.en.wikipedia.org/wiki/Videographer
- www.weva.com

Virtual Assistant

What You'll Do:
 As a virtual assistant, you'll be an administrative assistant who works in a home office. You'll use the internet, the telephone, and possibly a fax machine to communicate with, and transfer data to, your clients. You'll be like a long-distance receptionist. You may screen calls, take messages, return emails or telephone calls, fax memos, and perform other administrative duties.
 Prior experience in this field of work is usually recommended, though the only way to gain experience is by doing. As long as you're confident you can do the job, you could charge a low rate and accept minimal clients to gain experience before trying for more lucrative opportunities.

What to do with Your Children:
 Since you'll be performing duties that require your full attention, and handling communications that require professionalism, you should try to work when your children won't be distracting you or being heard in the background of telephone conversations. You could work while they're napping, at school, at sports practice, or being supervised in another room by your husband or another responsible caregiver.

Estimated Time Required:
 The time required will depend on the number of clients you have and how many hours they want you to work for them. There's no reliable estimate for the time required. It could be a few hours per day, week, or month, but it shouldn't be full-time unless you want it to be. Just accept and decline jobs based on the amount of time you want to spend working.

Estimated Income:
 At the time of this writing, a good estimate of income for virtual assistants is around $19 per hour, but your rates will depend on

your experience and the demand for your service. Just as an example, if you had 2 jobs per month that each required you to work 8 hours per week, at a rate of $19 per hour, you'd earn $1216 per month. That's just an example though. Your income will vary.

Estimated Investment Needed:
You will need a computer and internet access. You'll probably also need a telephone with long distance, and possibly a fax machine.

Advertising:
You could set up a website and register it with online search engines. You could also place an ad in the telephone book. To get started, you may want to search for jobs online.

Additional Information and Resources:
Some websites that you may find helpful for this business are listed below.
- www.CWAHM.com
- www.assistu.com
- www.mommysplace.net/become_a_virtual_assistant.html
- www.va-theseries.com
- www.magicjack.com

Website Content Writing

What You'll Do:
As a website content writer, you'll write relevant content for websites, generally for marketing purposes. You'll need to use keywords in the content that internet users may search for through search engines so that the website for which you're creating the content will be listed in the search results. The content you write should really engage the readers and entice them to become customers, subscribers, or members of the service or product that the website for which you're writing content is offering.

What to do with Your Children:
Since this is an online job, you could work from home anytime you have free time. You could work while your children are napping, in bed at night, at school, at sports practice, at a playdate, or even watching television or playing a game.

Searching online for copywriting jobs could be done anytime you are able to use the computer.

Estimated Time Required:
The time required will depend on the number of clients you have and how particular they are about the content. It will also depend on how quickly you think of the content and put it in text form. There's no reliable estimate for the time required, but it shouldn't be full-time unless you want it to be. Just accept and decline jobs based on the amount of time you want to spend working.

Estimated Income:
At the time of this writing, an estimate of income for freelance content writers is anywhere from $10 to $125 per hour. The amount you charge will probably depend on the demand for your services, but if you had 4 jobs per month that each required you to work 8 hours, at a rate of $20 per hour, you'd earn $640 per month. That's just an example though. Your income will depend on your rates, the number

of clients you have, and the number of hours you spend working on the projects.

Estimated Investment Needed:
You will need a computer and internet access. That should be about it.

Advertising:
You could email letters explaining your services to various website owners. You could place an ad in the telephone book. You could also set up a website if you'd like, and register it with online search engines.
To start out though, I recommend searching for jobs online.

Additional Information and Resources:
Some websites that you may find helpful for this income stream are listed below.
- www.ELance.com
- www.ScriptLance.com
- www.DailyFreelanceJobs.com
- www.HireMyMom.com
- www.FreelanceWriting.com
- www.workathomenoscams.com/work-from-home-companies

__Website Creation & Maintenance__

What You'll Do:
    You'll be responsible for creating websites using criteria provided by your clients. You'll also be responsible for maintaining the website as agreed upon by you and your clients. You'll make necessary changes and updates on the sites and be responsible for making sure the site is working properly.
    You'll be responsible for keeping the payments current to the hosting site and for terminating the websites that clients decide not to renew.
    Although this seems like a complicated business, by using a website template on a site such as www.FreeServers.com, it's actually pretty simple. At FreeServers.com, once you choose the website template, the site will be pretty much designed and formatted for you. All you'll need to do is enter the appropriate information in the areas specified for text, pictures, and contact information or links. You can change or edit it at any time, too.

What to do with Your Children:
    Since you'll want to focus on the websites you're creating, you might want to work on them while your children are napping, at school, or being supervised by your spouse. If you need a large block of time to create multiple websites, you could hire a babysitter if necessary.
    When meeting with clients, you shouldn't bring your children with you. Go to meetings when your children are at school, ask your husband to watch them, drop them off at their grandmother's house, or hire a babysitter.
    If your clients prefer to communicate by telephone and email rather than face-to-face, you can talk on the phone when your house is quiet and you can focus on what your client is telling you, perhaps during your children's naps or when they're at school. You can check

the emails from your clients anytime you can spare a few minutes, such as when the children are napping, at school, or even watching television.

If your children's ages have hit the double digits, they should be old enough to understand and comply when you tell them that you need privacy and/or quiet while you make a very important business call.

Estimated Time Required:
The time you spend working would depend on the number of clients you have, the website service you choose to use, your speed at creating websites, and the demands of your clients.

In general, you might spend up to an hour collecting information and specifications from a client. You will probably spend at least an hour creating a very simple site, and possibly days on more complicated sites.

Maintenance should be minimal, depending on the demands of your clients.

There is no reliable estimate for the amount of time you'll spend working, but only taking on projects that you feel comfortable with and not getting in too deep too fast should greatly reduce the time and stress involved in this business.

Estimated Income:
There is no reliable estimate of income for this business. It would depend on your rates, which will probably be based on the complexity of the site and the estimated maintenance involved, and the number of clients you have.

Though your results will vary, an example would be to have 2 new clients in one month who each want a website created and already have 3 clients for whom you do maintenance for. If the new sites are fairly simple, and you charge only $200 per website, that would generate $400. If you charge $35 per month per website to maintain the sites for your 3 current clients, that would earn you another $105. If you pay FreeServers.com $10 per month per site, including the new sites you create, you would be paying $50 for the 5 websites. So, $400 + $105 -$50 = $455 for one month of work. That's just an example though, Your income will vary.

Estimated Investment Needed:
You would need a computer with internet access. You'd also be responsible for the monthly fees for the websites you create at FreeServers.com or whatever site you choose to use to create your websites.

Advertising:
Hanging flyers in malls and other businesses, putting brochures in brochure racks, and leaving business cards at random locations would get the word out, and so would word of mouth.

You may also consider approaching business owners and asking them if they'd be interested in your services if you gave them a 50% discount for the first 6 months. Restaurants would be good businesses to approach for that since their websites would probably be as simple as a picture of their establishment, their hours of operation, their location and contact information, and their menu – all of which could even be on the same page.

You could also practice your skills by making free websites for friends who would then tell others about your business.

Additional Information and Resources:
For resources to make your websites, check out www.FreeServers.com, www.Webs.com, or search online for "free websites". Most of those sites will give you the option to have a free site with their advertisements on it or to pay a low monthly rate for a site with no ads. You'll want to choose the site with no ads. To make a profit, just charge your clients more than the site charges you.

Two additional websites you may want to check out are www.Elance.com and www.Scriptlance.com. You may be able to find jobs listed there to boost your experience. Payment rates vary, but may be negotiable.

Wedding Planning

What You'll Do:

As a wedding planner, you'll meet with engaged couples to discuss their desires for their wedding. You'll discuss the location, the color scheme, the music, the photographer, the menu, and all of the other details for the event.

You'll probably compile a portfolio of possible florists, caterers, bakers, musicians, and others who may be relevant to a wedding for the couple to browse through for options. You may accompany the bride to dress fittings. You may accompany the couple to bakeries to sample cakes. You may accompany the couple to tuxedo fittings. You will probably be involved in nearly every single aspect of the wedding you're planning. Some couples may only want limited involvement, but most will probably want practically the entire job done for them.

Once you have all of the information from the couples, you'll arrange the perfect day for them. You'll book the caterer, photographer, band, limousine service, reception hall, and everything else that needs taken care of.

You will be in charge of making sure that the day goes off without a hitch. Since planning a wedding can be very stressful, even though you won't be the bride this time, you can expect to run into some difficulties yourself. Wedding planning is definitely not a stress-free job.

Don't forget to get a deposit for the services you'll be booking for the couple. You certainly wouldn't want to have to pay out of pocket for them.

What to do with Your Children:

Since your clients deserve your full attention, it's best to meet with clients while your children are at school or being cared for by someone else. If they won't be a distraction to you, you could book the appropriate venues for the weddings at home even while your children are there.

Estimated Time Required:

There is no reliable estimate of time required for this business since every wedding is different. It will depend on the couples' desires for their weddings. Think back to your own wedding to get an estimate of the time involved.

Estimated Income:

Income varies greatly for this job. You'll charge either a percentage of the total cost of the wedding, a flat fee, or an hourly rate. Your income will depend on the number of clients you have, and probably the cost of the weddings, and the amount of time you spend planning them. Check around for the cost for wedding planners in your area, and offer a competitive rate.

Just as an example though, if you plan 12 weddings per year and earn $1,500 per wedding, your yearly income would be $18,000. The same amount of less costly $500 weddings would put your income at $6,000 per year. I used yearly income for the estimates because this business is seasonal. You'll probably plan many more weddings in some months than you will in others. Those are just examples though. Your income will vary.

Estimated Investment Needed:

You'll definitely need a telephone for all of the calls you'll need to make. You could work from home, but if you'd like to rent office space you could. Although you'll need to put a deposit on the services you reserve for the weddings, you could charge your clients up front for those expenses instead of paying out of pocket for them. The amount you spend to create your portfolio should be minimal.

This shouldn't be a very costly business to start.

Advertising:

I highly recommend placing an ad in the telephone book. You could also place an ad in the newspaper. You could leave business cards at flower shops, wedding dress boutiques, jewelry stores, tuxedo rental businesses, your local dry cleaners', party supply stores, bakeries, and any other businesses that may offer wedding products or services. You could also create a website for your business. If you wanted to advertise really big, you could rent a billboard.

Additional Information and Resources:

Some websites that you may find helpful for this business are listed below.

- www.EZWeddingPlanner.com
- www.weddingwire.com/shared/Rate
- www.DreamWeddingPlanner.com
- www.topweddingsites.com/become-a-wedding-planner.html
- www.fabjob.com/weddingplanner.asp

Wild Game Processing

What You'll Do:
 Processing wild game is like being a butcher. You may be able to negotiate whether or not the hides will be removed before processing, but generally, the hides are left on the animals when they're dropped off for processing.
 You'll need to ask your customers what cuts of meat they'd like or how they want their game prepared. They may want steaks, roasts, ground meat, stew meat, steak strips for making jerky, or some other cut. They'll probably request a combination of cuts. They'll also tell you how lean they want their meat.
 You'll be responsible for keeping the meat at a safe temperature, skinning the animal, cutting the meat off of the animal and into the customer's desired cuts, grinding the meat, packaging the meat, keeping your work area sanitary, disposing of the hide and carcass, collecting payment, and giving the meat to the customer.
 If your husband is a hunter, he may even want to help you with this business. If you've never processed your own meat before, you can buy a book on the subject or look online for instructions. Everyone who processes wild game has a first time, so don't worry about making a mistake. Just try processing game for your own family before you charge others for it.

What to do with Your Children:
 If your children have reached adolescence and are interested in hunting, they may be able to help. If not, you'll need to hire a babysitter or process the animals while your children are at school. The dead animals and blood may be frightening for some children. If you don't want your children to be exposed to those sights, make sure your work area is in an area where they can't see what's going on.

Estimated Time Required:

The amount of time needed for this business would depend on the number of customers you have, your speed at processing the animals, and mostly on the types of animals you'll be processing. Birds wouldn't take very long. Deer and wild boars would probably take a few hours or more, especially if you have to grind the meat. Larger game, such as elk or moose, could take all day. Those are just examples though. Your working hours will vary.

By specifying the types of animals you're willing to process, you can control the amount of time you spend working. If you're already as busy as you'd like to be, feel free to turn customers away. Tell them that you've got as many animals as you can process and that you don't want to risk having their meat spoil because you couldn't process it in a timely manner. By being honest and voicing your concerns about their health and safety, you'll appear caring and responsible and may get another chance to process their game from future hunts.

Estimated Income:

Your income will depend on the number of animals you process, the types of animals they are, and how much you charge for your services. At the time of this writing, in my area, the going rate for deer processing is around $75 per deer.

There is no reliable answer for the amount of money you'll make. It will probably vary from day to day, and it is a seasonal business so the income won't be year-round.

Estimated Investment Needed:

You may need to purchase processing equipment such as knives and a meat grinder. Your best bet would probably be to compare prices at Amazon.com for those items. There are wild game processing kits you can buy.

You'll need to buy freezer paper and tape to package the meat, and you'll need a marker to label the packages with the cuts they contain. You'll probably want cardboard boxes to put the processed meat in for the customer, but you can use any that you already have from buying food or diapers in bulk.

You may be required to purchase permits and/or licenses and have current food safety certification. The prices vary, so you'll need to check with the proper authorities regarding the requirements and fees for a wild game processing business.

If you don't have a spare freezer or refrigerator and the meat will be left with you longer than it would be safe to have it out of refrigeration, you may want to buy a spare refrigerator or freezer. If that investment would be too large for you, you could ask to borrow one from a friend, relative, or neighbor; or you could look for a free one on www.Freecycle.com.

Advertising:
You could hang flyers or leave business cards at lodges, motels, and sporting goods stores. Word of mouth would also be greatly beneficial.

Additional Information and Resources:
Check with your local government authority to find out the rules and regulations regarding a wild game processing business in your area.

Conclusion

I'm happy to say that I'm a full-time mom and a part-time author, and I hope that soon you can say you have a similar title.

On the following pages, you'll find a worksheet to help you determine what income stream(s) may best suit you. There's also a sample worksheet filled out for you as an example. Feel free to be as creative as possible.

Best wishes on your new income stream!

Personal Income Stream Assessment

1. What income streams in this book caught my eye? If I've previously tried any of them, why didn't they work out for me?

2. What income streams can I think of that aren't listed in this book?

3. What are my interests, and what skills and talents do I possess that I could use for the purpose of earning an income?

4. What have I helped others accomplish?

5. What do I receive frequent complements on?

6. What products or services do others pay for that I could do a better job of providing?

7. What products or services do we lack in our area that I may be able to provide?

8. What assets do I have that could help me earn an income?

9. What skills could I learn that could help me earn an income?

10. Am I willing to further my education or receive training?

11. Do I have childcare help if necessary? If so, at what times? Could I fit my work schedule into those times?

12. How much money do I want to earn?

13. What jobs could help me reach my financial goal?

14. Am I willing to invest money to start a business? If so, how much?

15. After careful thought and consideration, what income stream(s) do I believe would be best for me, and why?

Sample Personal Income Stream Assessment

1. **What income streams in this book caught my eye? If I've previously tried any of them, why didn't they work out for me?**

Baking restaurant desserts, MLM, sewing, HITs, real estate agent, coaching, fitness instruction, comic, direct sales

I tried selling cosmetics, but there was too much competition for that brand in my area. I tried mlms, but I got impatient.

2. **What income streams can I think of that aren't listed in this book?**

Crafts, jewelry repair, plumber, home inspector, pool cleaner, personal trainer, cartoonist, landscape company owner, professional organizer, baking Christmas cookies, storage rental units, dog grooming, taking others' clothes to dry cleaner

3. **What are my interests, and what skills and talents do I possess that I could use for the purpose of earning an income?**

Fast typing, good cook, baking, sewing, caring for children, attention to detail, very organized, I love fitness, nutrition, and health related things. I also like to tell jokes, and I'm pretty good at being funny.

4. **What have I helped others accomplish?**

vacation Bible school, budgeting, creating a meal calendar, starting a fitness routine, sticking to a diet

5. **What do I receive frequent complements on?**

how fit I am, how good my cooking tastes, what a good listener I am, how I'm a good leader

6. **What products or services do others pay for that I could do a better job of providing?**

a gym, body care products, window washing

7. **What products or services do we lack in our area that I may be able to provide?**
a dietician, aerobics classes, cooking classes, natural cosmetics, appliance repair

8. **What assets do I have that could help me earn an income?**
a car, a savings account, 3 acres of land, a computer

9. **What skills could I learn that could help me earn an income?**
A foreign language, medical billing and coding, investing strategies

10. **Am I willing to further my education or receive training?**
I'm willing to do online training, or training locally, if it's not very expensive and won't last a long time.

11. **Do I have childcare help if necessary? If so, at what times? Could I fit my work schedule into those times?**
My mother lives a couple minutes away, my husband has off work and can help me 2 days per week, and we have a babysitter we've used a few times that the kids like

12. **How much money do I want to earn?**
$300 per month would be nice

13. **What jobs could help me reach my financial goal?**
Probably all of the ones I listed above, like dietician, coaching, and being a real estate agent. Not sewing or HITs though.

14. **Am I willing to invest money to start a business? If so, how much?**
Yes, up to $1,000

15. After careful thought and consideration, what income stream(s) do I believe would be best for me and my family, and why?

I think conducting aerobics classes. I'd spend minimal time away from my children. I'd have a set schedule. I believe I can earn my monthly goal. I'd be setting a good example for my children of living a healthy lifestyle. I love to exercise anyway. And I found someone in my town who can certify me for a few hundred dollars with minimal training.

Additional Notes:

About The Author

Randi Lynn Millward resides in Marienville, Pennsylvania, with her husband, Travis, their two daughters, Aurora Joy and Mercy Kahlynn, and their son, Linkin Ryan. Randi is currently a full-time mom and a part-time author. She previously worked in the fields of childcare, restaurant services, and restaurant management, and was also self-employed as a housekeeper.

In addition to this book, Randi is the author of *Beyond the Traditional Lemonade Stand: Creative Business Stand Plans for Children of All Ages* and *50 Eggcellent Egg-Free Breakfast Recipes: Because People with Egg Allergies Deserve a Good Breakfast, Too!*, and her writing has appeared in the Business Builders section of the Christian Work At Home Moms (CWAHM) newsletter on more than a dozen occasions.

In 2004, Randi received a certificate in Creative Writing and Manuscript Marketing from Charter Oak State College of West Redding, Connecticut. In 2006, she received her ASB in Business Management with an option in Human Resources Management from Penn Foster College of Scranton, Pennsylvania.

To contact Randi or order additional copies of this book, or any other book that she's authored, visit her website at:

www.RandiLynnMillward.com